C000192867

Living with Grandma

A Hull woman recalls her childhood in Monmouth and the Rhondda

by

Lucy Arundell

Foreword by Ruth Madoc

Highgate Publications (Beverley) Ltd

1987

© Lucy Arundell, 1987

ISBN 0 948929 06 5

Published by Highgate Publications (Beverley) Ltd.
24 Wylies Road, Beverley, HU17 7AP
Telephone (0482) 866826

Cover design by Tina Green Creative Services
White Cottage, East Bank Road, Sunk Island

Photographs of Monmouth on pages 7, 15 and 45 reproduced by permission
of Monmouth Museum

Printed and Typeset in 10 on 11pt Baskerville by
B.A. Press, 2-4 Newbegin, Lairgate, Beverley, HU17 8EG
Telephone (0482) 882232

British Library Cataloguing in Publication Data

Arundell, Lucy
    Living with grandma: a Hull woman recalls her childhood in Monmouth and the
    Rhondda.
    1.   Wales, South — South life and customs
    I.   Title
    942.9'4083'0924   DA740.S65

ISBN 0-948929-06-5

Foreword

I read *Living With Grandma* with great interest. The story was almost *déjà vu* for me. Each page seemed to jog my memory of thirty years ago for, like the author, I was brought up by my mother's mother and her sister, Great Aunt Nan, the village midwife for most of her adult life. There was a lot of laughter in the 1930's-style house they shared, mainly because their observations of life were sharp and witty.

My favourite time of the day was early evening. Food and washing-up done, then to sit down and coerce out of them both the tales of gypsies, Flannel Fairs, maniac revolutionists, preachers, wild-cat strikes and the hushed tones of, 'Well, she had to get married, didn't she?' and, 'He was a bad lot'. All became firmly cemented in my young, very fertile imagination. And, although I had heard many of the stories before, they always seemed that little bit better for the next telling.

July 1987   **RUTH MADOC**

Preface

Fate must have decreed at the moment of my birth that for the next 26 years I should be moved around the country like a piece on a chess board. Instead of black and white squares it was towns and cities. From all the many places I have lived in there are four, each laying claim to a part of my heart. Hull, which is my adoptive city, Monmouth and Usk in Gwent, and the Rhondda Valley in South Wales.

My husband brought me to Hull with our five-months-old daughter. He had finished a six-year spell in the Army and wanted to settle down among his own folks in his native city. I did not blame him for that, but I was often unhappy and homesick. It was March 1939 and war was just around the corner. I longed for the peace and beauty of the home I had left.

Our lovely little girl did not stay long enough to grow up, but by 1951 we had three sons. For their sakes and because they were born here I decided to learn about local history and study Hull's beautiful historic buildings. In research I found a fascination and also a balm which soothed and quelled my longings. In time the place grew on me, I am here to stay but beg forgiveness if sometimes I still feel the old 'hiraeth'* and want to go and have another look at the places in the story.

Monmouth, the ancient town of great charm, steeped in history and its links with Agincourt: I picture with affection the house on the corner, my first remembered home. Then there is little Usk, home of my other grandfather and my ancestors from ages past. The Twyn Square has been made bigger by the removal of a row of old cottages, and new housing estates have of necessity sprung up, yet it seems not to lose its character. You can still find peace and tranquillity on the Island down by the fast-flowing river.

Bitterness cut deep into the soul of my grandmother. It made her so difficult to live with. I sometimes feel that she is leaning over me as I write, just as she did when I wrote my Christmas thank-you letters so long ago. I think she would have me tell you never to allow bitterness and hatred to rule your life. It can destroy you as surely as though you were cut down by a sword.

Hull June 1987   Lucy Arundell

*'hiraeth' is a word belonging to Wales and for which there is no exact translation: it represents all the longings a Welsh person has for Wales, especially if in exile. L.A.

2

Chapter 1

Grown-ups complicated everything. They kept on saying silly things like, 'Keep your frock clean', and 'Don't fidget'. The stupidest remark of all was the 'Look where you are going' one. This was usually accompanied by a prod in the back from a couple of bony fingers, or the sharp ferrule end of an umbrella from someone who followed on behind. Silly because, with my head well down, eyes rivetted on each forward movement of my black button-booted feet (brown on Sundays), I *was* looking where I was going. It was, of course, just my bad luck if during the process I bumped into someone, or ran my head into the edge of a half-open door.

Life with Grandma was far from easy. She had been born during the reign of Victoria, and had carried on right through the Edwardian and into the Georgian era, George the Fifth that is, keeping to the standards she had set for herself when at the age of seventeen she had met and married Grandpa and set up home in Monmouth. There was, she said, a place for everything and everything must be in its place. Her house was never upset or untidy like some of the houses we visited. All the work must be done in the morning. Afternoons were for resting. At least two hours lie-down was needed to gather up sufficient energy to face what was left of the day. It was a sensible arrangement when you consider that most evenings, weather and season permitting, we took long walks down country roads or visited friends.

Grandma had reared nine of her ten babies into strong healthy men and women. Quite an achievement in those days. Large families were the order of the day, but one never expected to get them all past the infant stage. It was probably due to her grim determination to see any task through to a successful conclusion, however difficult it might prove.

She was born into a simple country home. Her father was the village shoemaker, the living was very poor. Grandma felt that she had attained some degree of affluence in her marriage and looked forward to helping her mother in a practical way. Grandpa was twenty years her senior and had come across from Cork in southern Ireland with plenty of smart clothes and an old wooden chest containing a hoard of golden sovereigns. They must have been a striking pair. He had red-gold hair, tightly curled, beard, moustache and sideburns as was the fashion at that time. His forget-me-not blue eyes were in sharp contrast to hers, near black, flashing gypsy-like, matching her raven hair. She stood only four foot ten, had a seventeen-inch waist — or so she said — and feared neither man nor beast.

As her babies arrived in quick succession so the golden hoard dwindled until at last there was nothing left. Grandpa held a job as town postman for some years but in the end his sciatica beat him. After that he worked evenings as potman at the pub on the square. Grandma had a lot to say about that, mostly sarcastic. She felt it was very undignified, a base occupation. He worked as long as he was able, it put a shilling or two in his pocket and he enjoyed the pleasant company of those whom she described as his 'fancy women', his cronies.

I had been brought into the old house when I was two years old. Somewhere in the folds of my mind lay a misty memory. A half-forgotten picture of someone who had carried me along in his arms, played with me on a train journey, then walked me through the dark night to my new home. When I awoke the next morning he had gone. I was left to stumble along life's pathway under the auspices of my grandmother who never once let me forget that I was a very lucky girl to have found such a good home.

By the time I arrived there all Grandma's children had gone out into the world to make their own lives. All that is except Aunt Hilda who was fifteen years older than me. Grandpa was already an old man with snow-white hair and whiskers. His eyes came alive when he told me lurid tales of his imagination. Quite often I went to bed in a state of terror in case some monster lurking behind the huge wardrobe jumped out at me in the thick dark of night.

Now that Aunt Hilda was seventeen she put up her hair, sure sign that she was grown up. She had beautiful long shiny black tresses which she swept up from the nape of her neck to form a coronet on the top of her head. One morning, shortly after my arrival, instead of Grandma coming to wake me up, Aunt Hilda came. As she lifted me out of bed she said, 'You must be a good girl today. I'm looking after you. Your poor Daddy has gone to Jesus in Heaven to be an angel.' She tied a black ribbon in my hair. At such a tender age one has no preconceived ideas about Heaven. I suppose I accepted the statement, then put it from my mind.

Lucy's father, Arthur Edwin Knowles, born c.1880. Photograph taken approximately 5 years before he died, aged 35.

4

Suddenly, everybody wore long faces and black clothes. Handkerchiefs were black-bordered, as were the letters that came through the door. I was unaware of the personal tragedy, or even that we were not alone in this. It was late 1914 and, although our little market town was far removed from the war front, news was beginning to filter in. Sadness fell upon many families. It marked the turning point in Britain's history. Old values were to change, customs die away. People would take on a new way of life. It was, indeed, the end of an era.

Aunt Hilda brought in a tiny black and white kitten. 'It's for Lucy,' she said. Alas the poor thing was whisked away the following day, never to return. 'Naughty Lucy,' they said, standing over me while explaining certain facts of behaviour. 'You are a cruel little girl. Until you can learn how to treat an animal properly you can't have another one.' My bottom smarted from their chastisement and I really could not see what all the fuss was about. If only they had listened to me I could have explained the whole thing. That was their trouble, no one ever listened, or, if they did, they just snorted in disgust or laughed derisively when I said anything important. All I had done was offer the thing a drink. The water tap was far away above my reach so what better place to choose than the lavatory pan where there was always a good supply of water? I just held the kitten head first down into the bowl so that it could reach. That's when Aunt Hilda came in and immediately put the wrong conclusion on the affair.

When I was three years old Aunt Hilda packed up her belongings and went off to London to seek her fortune. 'There's nothing in this dead and alive hole for me,' she said. The young have been saying things like that since Adam was a lad, and no doubt will go on doing so. Grandma made her opinion of the matter known in no uncertain way: 'Going off up there! It's a city of iniquity, that's what it is. Women gadding about all over the place half naked. Up to no good, mark my words!'

Mystified and intrigued I wondered about these women. 'Why did they go around half naked? Weren't they cold like that?' I asked. 'What's a city of what you said, Grandma?' 'Don't ask silly questions. You wouldn't understand if I told you.' It was always the same. 'If you don't know, ask.' But when you asked all you got was, 'Don't ask! or, 'Little girls should be seen but not heard.'

I missed my aunt. Without her the house was too quiet, devoid of warmth and laughter. She was young and lively. Although I often got the sharp end of her tongue and little escaped her eagle eye, I liked her. I hoped that she might not like living in London and come back to us. She did not come back, but took to that great city like a duck takes to water and spent the rest of her life there.

There were to be no more long sleepy afternoons spent lying in cool grass, doing nothing more strenuous than gazing up at lambs'-wool clouds drifting across the summer skies. Gone too were the pleasant hours rowing up river with one of aunt's boy friends on the oars, her hand on the tiller. The boat was always left up river and we walked back home through the fields at water's edge. If I close my eyes and think about it, I can still feel the lush cool grass around my legs, see in my mind's eye the tall graceful marguerites swaying in the soft summer breeze. I smell again their fragrance as they nodded their heads to the fast flowing river. There are other, less pleasant memories of the River Wye. The thunderous roar of brown muddy waters, swollen in flood, rushing along through low-level streets, destroying as it went its relentless way.

Aunt Kate, on Grandma's side of the family, always seemed to be working. The house, at least the kitchen and yard — had numerous buckets standing around with washing, pickles or even whitewash. I never saw the place tidy. She had three little boys. The eldest, Jackie, who was the same age as me, had a revolting habit of keeping minnows in a bucket. I felt quite sickened as he demonstrated his skill in pushing a thumb through the unfortunate fish's gills to bring it out of its mouth. I lay awake in bed at night suffering its agonies and wondering how long a fish could stand up to that kind of treatment before it expired.

The boys were very fond of playing on the river's edge. I went with them one summer evening. Grandma removed my boots and socks so that I could paddle in as well. The stony beach was difficult to walk upon, I stood hesitantly at the water's edge. Someone gave me a hefty push from behind and said, 'Go on! Get in !' Taken completely by surprise I toppled over and fell flat on my face in the river. I was lifted out and scolded for making such a fuss. 'Nothing to cry about, you little ninny,' they said.

My distress was genuine, not only had I seen visions of death by drowning — for how many times had I been told not to go too near the river in case I fell in. To add to my shock, I was soaked through to the skin and my hair hung bedraggled over my face. It may be as a result of that early experience that I have never scraped up the courage to do more than wet my feet carefully when everyone around me was leaping about among the waves, enjoying their seaside holidays.

6

Chapter 2

Monmouth was an ancient country market town. We lived near to its heart. Our three-storied house stood on a corner. The back door opened into the side street, St. John's, while from the front windows we could look right along the larger Glendower Street which led straight down to the riverside. The houses were not of uniform size, but rather gave one the impression of having being built at different periods — and small ones were sandwiched between larger grander houses, almost like an afterthought. For all this seemingly odd fashion, the buildings blended in well together and never appeared out of proportion.

Front doors were expressive of an age of dignity. Stout and yet simple in design, always kept well washed and polished. Brass or bronze letter boxes and knockers shone and sparkled in the morning sunlight. Footscrapers were commonly used, either ornamental in the style of a horse or lion rampant as at the top of the steps of the larger houses. In the case of small houses or cottages these were usually built into the walls at pavement level near to the front doors. No one in those days ever took muddy shoes or boots into the house without first using the scraper.

There was very little activity along the street, except in early morning when steps were washed, mats shaken and, if need be, pavements swilled. For a while doors would stand open to reveal interiors. Should

Agincourt Square, Monmouth, in 1914. Beyond is Priory Street and the New Market Hall.

there be a passer-by, he or she might catch a glimpse of long passages, doors with richly coloured glass panels half open to the garden beyond, from where the scent of roses or lilac came drifting through on the cool morning air. The doors would close and the occupants be lost to view until such time that they came out to go about their business or do the shopping.

It was quite a different matter however when there was a race meeting or it was time for the Assizes. Then the whole town would come alive and fill with strangers. Beautiful horses were paraded around the streets to cool off after their gruelling races on the course in the fields by the river. At Assizes time the place would be buzzing with gossip. Prisoners were sometimes brought in from the prison — the nearest was twelve miles away. I remember a very young man being brought up for murder. He was of course convicted and sentenced to death. I was afraid that he might escape before the police got him safely back to prison. Grandma described to me in great detail all the court procedure. I don't know whether she had ever attended a trial in person but she always seemed to know about such matters, even about the black cap worn by the judge when he pronounced sentence of death.

Grandpa had an allotment. It was too far for me to visit regularly being about three miles away from the town. I would have liked to have gone when I became old enough to make the journey but Grandma was not in favour. We were never short of fresh vegetables and the house was fragrant with bunches of flowers he brought in. I think the neighbours were sorry for the little girl without a garden to play in, for I was often invited into theirs. In particular, Mrs. Gray's. She was a widow with a son to bring up and she kept a boarding house for business gentlemen. I liked it there, it was a warm overgrown jungle of a place where parsley, mint and nasturtiums ran riot while roses rambled their way through neglected fruit bushes. Sitting there on the sun-warmed wooden bench, to me the glass of milk and the slice of bread and jam seemed to taste so much better than anything I ever had at home.

Being in some way related to the local undertaker, I sometimes went to play with his little son. Henry was only three years old, I was six. We got on famously together and romped and laughed among knee-high wood shavings in the workshops. I have always loved the smell of new wood. No one ever came and said, 'Stop that,' or 'Don't make so much noise,' nor did it seem odd to us that we should play among an assortment of coffins in various stages of construction.

As winter approached, summer curtains and bedding were replaced with darker heavier counterparts to make everything cosy within during the long cold months. At this time, too, floors, and all the heavy oak and mahogany furniture smelled of beeswax and turpentine and were in mirror-like condition. Cleaning was always done at the out-set of autumn and again just before Easter when the order of things was reversed.

In 1915 I already knew a few lines of some of the popular songs, *Charlie Chaplin* and *Tipperary*. I had a Charlie Chaplin doll with a short body, bent legs and feet a-splay. I loved him dearly, but sadly the day came when he began to shed his sawdust filling about the floor. Grandma could not stand any mess and relegated him to the flames of the open fire. Charlie made a wonderful blaze as sparks from his broken body crackled and danced up the chimney back. Someone gave me a beautiful china doll in replacement but I never forgot my dear Charlie.

For as long as I can remember I have been interested in books. I spent hours poring over the pictures. There were many missionary books along the bookshelves and those pictures frightened me somewhat. I was horrified at the way these strange fuzzy-haired people stuck bones through their noses and lips and practised other tortuous modes of dress. My favourite book was *Pilgrim's Progress*. I sat enthralled at Grandma's feet while she read a chapter to me before bedtime. When she was too busy I just looked at the pictures, building up in my mind over and over all that I could recognise and remember of the story. Although I did not always understand what was being read, I would pick some word that fascinated me by its sound and roll it around on my tongue repeatedly.

Perhaps I was asking too many questions or being difficult, but at three and a half years of age I had been sent to school. With a new dress, new button-up boots and new under-clothing, it looked as though school was going to be an interesting venture. Grandma took great pains to stress the fact that, as I was now a big girl, she would no longer be in attendance when nature required. Suddenly it seemed that I was entering the world of the grown-ups and going to have to do a lot of things for myself from now on. Most importantly, I must not forget to ask Teacher to excuse me when I needed to leave the room.

School fell far short of my expectations. I quickly found out that, strict and severe as Grandma was, here was another, if anything, more formidable, person to deal with. Teacher was very old, a grey gaunt figure who did not suffer fools gladly at any level. The building was solidly constructed of grey stone. Small windows set high in the walls kept the inmates secure from distraction by passers-by. The Infants' classroom to which I was directed differed from the rest in that its desks were tiered on steps. Teacher could see at a glance what anyone of us was up to at any moment. Sweets passing from hand to hand beneath desks were quickly seen and confiscated.

In winter a large coal fire burned brightly, conveniently near to Teacher's desk. For the children up at the top end of the room it might not have been there at all for all the good it did them. Most of us went home at teatime, our hands numb with the cold. I longed for the warm days of summer to come. The ages of the Infants' class ranged from three to four years. All were treated alike, to be taught whether they wanted to or not. Most of us at that tender age did not, but faced with the thought of punishment many managed to do remarkably well. It was the age of fear!

Justin Evans lived next door to us and he had been persuaded to bring me home, much to his displeasure. He was older than me and up into Primary class. He walked with me to school in the morning, then home again at dinner time. Well, part of the way. Alas, in spite of all Grandma's warnings I had been too scared to ask to leave the room during class time. Unable to contain myself any longer, I unfortunately disgraced myself there on the street. My mortification knew no bounds. Matters were not improved by Justin's behaviour either. He looked at me with disgust and loathing, then raced home as fast as he could. As he passed our front door he told the world, 'Lucy's piddled her britches.' Grandma was waiting on the doorstep. Before I met my bed that night I had learnt some more words. 'Shameless hussy', 'Dirty disgrace', and, 'If you ever do that again the tanning you've had today is nothing to what you'll get next time, my lady.'

Justin did not call for me again. I was much relieved. His mother took in sewing, and their little house was sandwiched between our larger one and the old disused jail. Grandma took me in there sometimes. I hated it, the place always smelt. Mrs.Evans would be 'pickling' onions or the baby would be sick, I could never get out of the stifling atmosphere quickly enough. Grandma said we should be sorry for Mrs. Evans, cooped up in a little place with two children while her brave husband was away fighting the Germans. I'm afraid I never harboured any such gracious thoughts.

Chapter 3

The first term at school came and went. We'd been learning the alphabet from coloured pictures pinned on the walls. Counting was done on frames of brightly coloured beads. I liked the colours but had a struggle to master the usage. I never have been any good at figures. Clay modelling was not bad but I hated getting the wet gooey stuff on my hands. Try as I would, I never achieved a masterpiece. Other girls and boys could produce a recognisable object, cat, dog or some other thing, but my efforts never produced any definable creation.

About half way through the second term slates and slate pencils were introduced. Teacher said — rather too gleefully, I thought, 'Now we shall see who has been paying attention and who has been dreaming.' Her gaze was directed at me and my face went bright red while my hands sweated. Paying attention was the key-word, but I could not help daydreaming. It was a kind of game played inside one's head when things became too difficult to understand.

Teacher wrote words on the blackboard for us to copy on to our slates. As we bent laboriously over our lesson she walked up and down between the rows of desks, sponge in hand to erase mistakes. The same method was applied in the case of sums. I made a fair representation of the words, but when it came to numbers I had my slate wiped off until there was little left to see. Then it was a case of, 'Lucy Knowles, stand out in front by my desk.' This was standard treatment for all dunces. Teacher had taught my aunts and uncles way back in time. 'They,' she said, 'were very clever', and she demanded to know why I could not be more like them.

Punishment came in the form of a hard thwack across the palm of the hand with Teacher's ruler, a hard rounded weapon which also served as a pointer for the blackboard. If she was feeling extra angry our hands were turned over and held as in a vice to rap us across the knuckles. This ensured that the offender was incapable of doing any further work that day, especially if the hands were blistered with chilblains — a regular winter-time affliction.

Through all these trials and tribulations, to say nothing of aching hands, I emerged from Infants at the end of my first school year and was all set to go up to Primary after the holidays. It was during the holidays that I decided not to go to school any more. I might have known that Grandma's views on the subject would be very different. 'Not go back to school, indeed! Rubbish! You'll go back alright, my lady, or I'll know the reason why!'

Something must have stirred within her at that point, for it was then that she decided to teach me to read. Among all the heartaches and disappointments that attended my long journey through schooldays this was the one great decision which brought joy to my heart. Grandma showed remarkable patience and a hitherto-unknown forbearance as she guided me through the works of John Bunyan, the Bible and her weekly Christian magazine. By the time school reopened for the new term I had begun to know and master a little of this wonderful new world. The world of words! I found that I now had a headstart on some of the other children when it came to reading lessons. This provided me with a newly-found and much-needed confidence. I was not such a dunce after all.

Compared to Infants' class, Primary was a happy place to be in. Our teacher, Miss Crawford, was young and lively. Mistakes were not nearly so severely dealt with here; consequently fewer occurred. I liked Miss Crawford from that moment when, marking the register, she paused to look at me and said, 'My name is Lucy, too.' I was hers for ever.

One morning Miss Crawford did not come to school. No one seemed to know why, or what to do about it. Mrs. Graham, the head teacher, came in and told us to look at our books quietly for a little while. Later Miss Jones from Standard Two came to take us in lessons. Miss Jones was older than Miss Crawford. She had a thin face and frizzy hair. Her reputation had, however, travelled before her. It was well known that she favoured regular use of a cane. The fact struck terror to our young hearts. We need not to have worried, though, she never caned any one in Primary. She was probably so used to dealing with older children and felt a bit out of her depth with us.

We did not get away altogether, however. Miss Jones adopted an air of severity in keeping with her long face and thin lips. She used her tongue to good effect and nagged us along to the end of the day. Nor did her eagle eyes escape the fidgety, the slow, or those who seemed to have their minds set on things far removed from the task in hand. Tilly Morgan sat next to me; she said in play-time, 'Don't she go on? She's worse than my Dad and he's bad enough.' Having no first-hand experience of Dads I could not comment apart from agreeing about the 'goings on'.

Dinner time, and we all rushed out, eager to relate the strange happenings to those at home. Parents and others could not help solve the mystery of Miss Crawford's non-appearance at school. The afternoon went by in much the same way, and we went home still hoping that tomorrow our dear Miss Crawford would turn up and explain all. Sadly, this was not to be. The next day turned out to be a memory milestone for us. Mrs. Graham brought the dreadful news. She looked very upset, and, as for Miss Jones, she just sat at her desk and seemed to have been overcome by a shocking cold and kept wiping her face with her hanky. I felt that something was wrong, I dare say the rest of the children felt that way too. People do not give children credit for their feelings. Grown-ups seem not to understand that children will very quickly pick up an atmosphere.

After a few whispered words with Miss Jones, Mrs. Graham turned to face the class. Her voice unusually quiet, she said, 'Children, I have some very sad news to tell you. Yesterday morning while Miss Crawford was riding to school on her bicycle she had a dreadful accident. The road was being repaired and it was muddy. Poor Miss

Crawford skidded and fell into the path of a steam-roller. She was taken to hospital where the doctor tried his best to save her life, but last night she died from her injuries.' A pause while we digested this, then Mrs. Graham began again: 'Now, children, Miss Crawford was a very kind and thoughtful lady, we are all going to miss her so much. She was fond of you all and told me that she was proud of the work you were doing. Now, I'm going to put you all on your honour to go on doing your best just as she would have wished. Miss Jones will look after you for the time being. Show her just how good you all can be.'

She left the classroom while Miss Jones continued to blow her nose, wipe her face and sniff. It was then I realised that other people liked Miss Crawford, too, not just me. She had been one of the special people we come across from time to time. They appear like bright stars across our vision, then fade suddenly and are gone for ever.

Miss Jones pulled herself together and lessons got under way, although in rather a quiet manner. No one seemed to want to talk. Play-time too was a rather subdued affair. We stood around in groups; the boys started a game of rounders, then abandoned the idea. Elsie Evans cried long and loud until Georgie Thomas said, 'Elsie, shut up!' Elsie, hanky in hand, always ready for an excuse to weep, replied morosely, 'She'll be put in a hole. How'd you like to be put in a hole and never see people any more?' We all associated death with burial and graves. After all, what was a grave but a hole in the ground? There was no other logical answer so we let the matter drop.

I supposed that it wouldn't be long before someone mentioned Jesus and Heaven. Sure enough, at home time Miss Jones said, 'Hands together, eyes closed, we will all say a very special prayer for dear Miss Crawford before we go home.' The prayer went on a bit, but we stood quietly until with some relief we could sing our vesper, *Lord keep us safe this night,* and hurry home. The news had by this time got around the town, people were shocked to hear the extent of Miss Crawford's injuries. The steam-roller driver was so upset that the Corporation had to give him a few days off work and try to find him some other kind of work for he said he could never ever drive again.

During the morning of the next day Mrs. Graham came into the classroom again. This time with news of the funeral: 'Miss Crawford is to be buried on Friday afternoon. If any of you would like to help to buy a wreath from this class, come and see me in my office. I will place a box on the desk for you to put your coppers in. Don't bring more than a penny, your mothers have enough to do with their money as it is. In fact a halfpenny will do very well. If you can't bring anything, don't worry. No one will know. A wreath will go in your name just the same.'

For the remainder of that day Miss Jones was rather quiet. She was still having trouble with her nose and eyes. Sometimes she spoke so softly we had difficulty in hearing what she had to say. I made my usual mess during clay-modelling, got much of the stuff on my dress and daubed about the desk. Tilly Evans broke her wooden clay knife and Georgie Thomas accidentally knocked over the vase of flowers on Teacher's desk as he passed. Miss Jones just said, 'Never mind. Go fetch a floorcloth from Mrs. Graham's room.' No shouting! No fuss!

Chapter 4

Miss Jones had prayed that Miss Crawford might rest in Heaven until we all met again one day. This idea of meeting again in Heaven caused my innocent mind to do a lot of searching. For the life of me I could not see how it was going to work. Heaven was a remote 'somewhere' up in the sky. People spoke of it frequently. They seemed to believe that that was where we should all end up if we were good and did what it said in the Bible. My question was, if all the people alive now were going to meet up with all the people who were already there, then Heaven was going to have to be a mighty large place.

It was all a bit beyond me. I tackled Grandma about it. She said we should be drawn up from the four quarters of the earth on Judgement Day. The good would go to Heaven and sit at the foot of God's throne. The wicked would go to Hell-fire and Damnation. There would be weeping and wailing and gnashing of teeth. I think she found great joy in repeating these passages from the Bible. She obviously gave no thought to the fact that the young are very impressionable. But children then were expected to listen to their elders and accept what they were told. To question the statements of a grown-up, however dramatic, was simply not done. Blind faith was all that was required of one.

Nevertheless, I worried secretly about many things which as yet I could not understand. Grandma explained that we were not supposed to understand everything, which did nothing to dispel my fears. For instance, suppose that I should not be accepted into Heaven, what then? How would I be able to bear the dreadful Hell-fire and Damnation, whatever that was? Perhaps if I had been raised within a happy family circle I would not have given a second thought to these overwhelming problems. Instead, I was a child alone and lonely, with too much time to think.

The School Board, that remote Body with power to say Yea or Nay, granted the school a half-day holiday for Friday afternoon so that we might, if we wished, pay our last respects to Miss Crawford. It was always nice to have a holiday, however it might have been arrived at. Grandma said, 'Stand in the Square by the new grocer's. You'll be able to see the funeral from there. Don't get in anyone's way and come straight back home after.'

It had been raining steadily all the morning but as the cortege came into view and began to cross Agincourt Square a shaft of sunlight broke through the clouds to dance across the waving black plumes of the horses' head dresses. They turned away on the last sad stage of the journey to the cemetery and I stood quietly watching the beautiful black animals, coats like polished satin. With measured steps they drew the hearse and covered carriages. The coffin was almost hidden beneath a blanket of wreaths. I was not close enough to see the one which we had sent from school but I knew it would be there.

Friday was market day. Stalls were piled high with goods on the cobble-stoned square. Wonderful wares were displayed there week by week. Out of respect for the funeral procession the stalls had been covered over, the holders stood with bared heads beneath the cloisters of the Town Hall. Here too stood the farmers' wives with their dressed poultry, eggs and pats of golden butter wrapped in cabbage leaves to keep cool.

Agincourt Square, Monmouth, in 1914. A statue commemorating the aviator C. S. Rolls stands in front of the Shire Hall. On the right, Monmouth's main street, Monnow Street, runs down toward the River Monnow and a mediaeval fortified bridge.

15

Life must go on! As soon as the last carriage had disappeared around the corner, off came the covers and the whole place sprang into action. I lingered on to watch the traders, for where else in the world but a market place could you see such acts of sheer magic performed? A man throwing a dozen dinner plates into the air and deftly catching them without so much as chipping, let alone dropping one. Or another man banging away at a watch defying all the laws of the universe proving that its glass could not be broken. This fascinated me so much that I waited quite a long time in the hope that sooner or later that crashing hammer would at last smash the watch. It never did. I guess those men had more than a few tricks up their sleeves when it came to hood-winking a gullible public.

One stall holder displayed a dummy head with rich brown tresses of hair. Alongside he had a little stove or charcoal burner into which he put small metal rods. He would then take a comb and quickly comb and wind the hair around hollow rollers which he then secured with hair pins. Next he would take the rods from the stove and allow them to cool slightly before pushing one into each roller. He never stopped talking, demonstrating how easy it all was. Then, while the hair was cooling, he went among the people with his wares, tins of solid brilliantine, bay rum and other requisites. By the time the sales were completed or no one in the crowd seemed anxious to part with any more money, the eager demonstrator stepped back up into his stall and removed rods and rollers from the hair of the dummy. He had the crowd spellbound as he combed out the hair and let it fall into fat ringlets. It all looked so easy, he invited the ladies to come forward and partake of this special offer of a pack of rollers *etc.* at half-price, only for this week, mind. They could, he said, attain such standards of beauty in the privacy of their own room. I have often wondered if any of the women who purchased kits ever achieved anything like the magnificent results demonstrated by that clever salesman.

Apart from these weekly pedlars who plied their wares on the Square, there were many others. Annual hawkers and tradesmen. One usually knew to within a day or so when to expect a visit. Blunted knives were put out ready for the knife grinder who worked his sharpening device from the wheel of his bicycle. Tinkers came to fix a washer in the hole in your saucepan or teapot or anything else which might have sprung a leak. You didn't go out and buy new things in those days, a penny would put another year on the life of most items.

Johnny Onion came from Brittany with necklaces of golden onions. You bought a string and hung it in the pantry, cutting off one whenever needed. They were delicious with a bit of crusty home-made bread and a hunk of cheese. Another regular visitor was the salt man, his cart loaded up with large blocks of salt. It cost sixpence a block until inflation reared its ugly head. Grandma said in no uncertain fashion that it was scandalous. The poor man tried to explain that it was because of the war. She would not listen to such rubbish and he needn't call next year. She would make this block last twice as long.

Salt blocks were sawn into smaller pieces, each well wrapped in newspaper to absorb any dampness. It was my job to produce fine salt for the table salt cellars. This was done by first drying out a piece overnight, breaking it into halves and rubbing these together over a warm plate. A stone jar would be filled up with rough pieces and kept handy in the kitchen for general cooking purposes and for cleaning down. I was taught that salt is a great cleanser and disinfectant, and have seen country women and farmers' wives scouring out their great stone sinks until they were as clean as on the day the stone-mason carved them out.

Gypsies came around to our door about twice each year. Grandma always bought something, even if it was only a few clothes' pegs. There was a superstitious idea that if you sent a gypsy woman away empty-handed she would lay a curse upon you and your family. A poor old tramp called at our house one Christmas day. He must have thought we were well off, living in a nice three-storied house in the quieter part of town. Grandma put fresh tea into his battered old enamel billy-can and I handed him a slice of Christmas cake. He thanked me, touching the brim of his hat and half bowing in respect. I am sure that if the truth had been known he would have much preferred a hunk of good old bread and dripping.

We did not see many tramps except in the winter when the weather drove them into the towns for shelter. Tramps in those days were not idle people living off the workers. They were mostly decent folk fallen on hard times. Traversing the country end to end, they took what work they could find, mending hedges, cleaning out ditches for farmers in return for a night's shelter and a little food. Although there seemed to be little or no security in this kind of existence, at least they kept their pride. They supported themselves in the best way they could, thus warding off the evil day when they would at last have to go into the workhouse to live on charity until they died, unwanted and unloved.

Chapter 5

By the time the year 1916 arrived the war was being more forcibly felt in many ways than before. At first it had been a matter of mainly hearsay, whose husband had been lost in battle, whose son had just gone to the Front. Suddenly it erupted within our very midst. No one now could avoid being caught up in it.

Soldiers arrived in their hundreds to rest up in the Grammar School gymnasium, the only place in the town which was large enough to convert into temporary barracks. People generally had referred to the fighting forces as 'those poor soldiers' and told and retold awful tales of the horrors experienced on the fields of Flanders. Gassing, shellshock, and other hitherto undreamed-of things became a part of the daily language. These soldiers, however, were a jolly lot. They laughed and joked and sang as they set about making the place habitable. Tables, chairs, benches and beds were brought out on to the cobble-stoned pavement to be scrubbed with tremendous vigour. Perhaps the commanding officers felt the same as Grandma about idle hands and Satan. They certainly kept those men busy.

While the men ate and slept in the barracks, some of the officers found private billets around the town. Others, of lesser rank no doubt, having to sleep where their men were, were offered whatever hospitality householders could provide. Parlours and best sitting rooms were opened up to allow the young men a place to sit and write their letters, have a sing-song around the piano, or a fry-up on the fire. Grandma handed over her Holy-Of-Holies, the 'little sitting room', and provided them with a huge frying pan wherein sausages, bacon and bread could be fried up for supper. Three young officers came to our house. A tall thin one, Wilkinson, ginger-headed Scotty, and a quiet shy one called Andy. I was well warned in advance to keep out of their way. 'Soldiers,' said Grandma, 'didn't want children hanging around. They wanted a bit of peace and quiet.' In spite of this I usually ended up on someone's lap having a dip into whatever the frying pan contained, before I was chased off to bed. Bed was up two flights of stairs well away from the 'little room', but I lay there listening to the songs they sang.

I can't remember how long the soldiers were stationed there, but sooner than expected, according to hearsay, they all marched away one sunny morning, singing as they went, uniforms immaculately pressed and buttons and cap badges gleaming. 'Poor young things, only boys some of them,' said Grandma. 'Just fancy, some of them might never come home again.' That profound statement was a sad reflection on the earlier prediction that, 'They'd all be home for Christmas,' when the first lot of bright-eyed eager young men went off to defend the honour of King and Country. The house was very quiet after the soldiers had gone. Grandma had a good clean-up and put everything back to its rightful place. By the time she had finished you'd never have known anyone had been there.

One morning a most peculiar rumbling sound was heard. Investigation showed this to be coming from a huge tank. 'Come straight from the Front,' someone said. It trundled along the street and settled outside the gymnasium. We had a grandstand view of everything that happened there because we were situated on the corner right next to it. I was very surprised to see a soldier coming head first through a hole in the top of the tank. Pictures of army tanks had appeared in all the newspapers but there were many people who did not buy a paper. To them and the rest of us it was a great and wonderful machine. A group of people quickly gathered around to explore the mechanism of the great tracks by which it was propelled along the ground.

A Red Cross nurse came out of the barracks to meet it in and joined the driver at the foot of the steps. She told us that our brave men were desperately short of many things: medicine for the wounded, bandages, clothes and weapons. On February 21 she told us, the Government had started a new kind of savings scheme by which we could all help our men. Holding aloft some small pieces of paper she went on to explain: 'These are Savings Certificates, and they will be your receipts for every sum of 15/6 that you give to us. When the war is over you will be able to hand these in and claim your money. Not only will you get back your contributions but each certificate will carry an extra bonus. You see, the Government will pay you interest for lending them your money.' Everybody was listening. 'If you leave them in until 1922 you will get back not just 15/6 but £1.0.6d.' The money we gave today, she said, would go straight into the funds for the soldiers. Judging by the number of people who climbed the steps to look down into the depths of the tank, then accepted a certificate on the way out, the Government should have been mighty pleased with the day's takings.

I don't suppose for one minute that it could ever have entered the head of the nurse or her companion that this was the start of something big. To them as to everybody else it was simply a wartime expediency; yet it has proved to be a most popular and easy way of saving, particularly for those who have little to spare. The scheme is still going strong in the last quarter of the twentieth century.

The ladies of the sewing parties who regularly met in drawing rooms and vicarages had put away their pretty embroideries and embarked on something known as Comforts for the Troops. They knitted socks, scarves, gloves and balaclavas by the hundreds. All in khaki coloured wool and all destined to keep at least a little warmth in the bodies freezing in the hell-holes of war.

A soup kitchen was set-up — in the gymnasium — for the poor. Anyone who wished might take a basin in and have it filled with a share of the rich brown stew. I asked Grandma for a basin, but, when I told her what I intended doing with it, she quickly poured scorn on that idea. 'Certainly not! We are not paupers, we do not require charity, thank you!' I thought it was a great pity. Having smelt the wonderful concoction I had been filled with a hunger the like of which I had never before experienced. She was rigid on decisions. I knew it would be useless to ask again. Her fierce pride never allowed her to do even the things which might have benefited us.

It must have been a tremendous struggle: I now realise that we were on the point of starvation. We lived rent free, which I was unaware of at that time, because the first floor rooms were used by the local workingmen's club. Grandma saw to it that the rooms were always clean and comfortable and fires lit in winter. When the club held its annual dinner or a smoking concert she would be in charge of catering and wait upon the company. As for actual money, all that came into the house was Grandpa's old-age pension which was ten shillings per week. That princely sum had to keep the three of us. My mother was quite unable to support me in any way.

Sometimes when Grandpa felt well enough he would do a few basket repairs or make a basket for someone. This was after he had had to give up the public house work through his chronic sciatica. Basket makers were once as much a part of daily life as is the shoe repairer. Grandpa was quite expert in the craft. I often stood watching him, fascinated by the way he could weave the cane or willow so deftly in and out with just two tools to his trade. A sharp knife for cutting and trimming and a short heavy implement which looked like a chisel with a pointed end to neaten the rows of the pattern as he went along. He had made a small basket for me, because, he said, I liked to play with the baskets brought in for repair and made such a fuss when the owners called to collect them. That was a treasured possession, later passed on to my own little girl. After she died I did not feel that I could bear to pass it on to another child and it now resides in a museum just around the corner from where it was first

The family home in Agincourt Street, Monmouth.

made all those years ago. It is a tribute to Grandpa's craftsmanship that it is still in excellent condition.

As time went by, Grandpa was so crippled with sciatica that he found it difficult to come downstairs. He sent me to the chemist's to buy a bottle of acetic acid which he rubbed vigorously into the aching limbs, swearing that it was doing him good. I am quite sure it was useless and it smelled awful. Although as I grew older I was allowed to carry out small errands like this for Grandpa, he was not really supposed to speak to me in the ordinary way. One day he forgot himself at the dinner table. Grandma arose and promptly smacked him hard across the mouth. 'How dare you speak to an innocent little child?' she said angrily. I was very shocked. I was quite used to being reprimanded. My bottom was often sore from hidings and my legs carried red weals where her cane had been used. This, however, was much different.

The vehemence of the swift action terrified me. Grandpa quietly got up from his chair and went upstairs. He did not stand up to her, never had to my knowledge. Perhaps he had in times past but found it to no avail and given up the struggle. It was such a sad way for two old people to live. They had brought all those children into the world but nothing now was left between them except bitterness.

Chapter 6

Sunday was a day of rest. That meant many extra jobs had to be carried out on Saturday. Early in the morning the living room fireplace had to be thoroughly cleaned out, flues swept, and the oven prepared to take the joint and a pudding later in the day. These would be eaten cold on Sunday regardless of the season. This was all in accordance with the Holy Laws which said that the Sabbath was the Lord's Day. No housewife need make the excuse that she was too busy to go to worship on Sunday mornings.

The room would be thoroughly swept out and dusted before lighting the fire. Grandma could not do with anyone hanging around while she was working so I usually played in the draughty stone-flagged hall and passage, even when winter came. I've never been much good in winter, cold weather has always made me miserable, and the damp floors sent a chill through my whole body. Cold and miserable, I cried. On one such occasion Grandma came out to ask what I was snivelling about now. At my reply, 'I'm cold,' she upended me and smacked my bottom hard. 'There now,' she said. 'That'll give you something to cry about! Warm you up as well!' Standing there in the lowest depths of misery I must have made a picture of abject despair.

There was a knock on the front door. Grandma shouted to me, 'See who it is and tell them I'm busy.' I managed to get the heavy door open and there standing on the step I saw what I could only imagine was an angel. No golden hair, though, no white robe or feathery wings like the angels in my picture books. She wore a long heavy coat with an armband that said G.P.O., a black hat and woolly gloves. There was something in her eyes as they met mine that conveyed a warmth, I could not know that it was love, I only knew it made me feel good.

The angel stooped down and kissed me, then with her large white hanky wiped away my tears. In the most beautiful voice I had ever heard she said, 'Don't cry, dear. Wait there a minute, then we'll go and buy some lollies.' That was the local name for sweets. I had no way of knowing what went on between the women behind that closed door. When she emerged she put my hat and coat on for me, took my hand and walked me out to the shops, warming my hands in hers as we went along.

The promised sweets were bought after a visit to the chemist's shop where she also bought some special medicine which had been out of stock at her local shop. But for this necessary train journey she would not have called at Grandma's house. As we neared our part of the street she said, 'I have to go away again, but don't cry any more. I'll come and see you very soon.' Another kiss and she left me on the doorstep. I watched and waved until she was out of sight. Grandma was unusually quiet for the rest of the morning. When at last she ventured to speak she said with some irritation and annoyance, 'Trust her to come poking her nose in. Never a by-your-leave or letting me know she was coming.' I put my question, 'Who was she?' The reply quite astonished me, but thrilled me too: 'Why, you stupid little ninny, she's your mother! Didn't you know that?'

That is how I discovered that I had a mother. The revelation made a great difference to me, and gave me such a lot to think about. I was on a level with all the other children who constantly talked about their fathers and mothers. My father was in Heaven. I could never see him. I accepted the fact without question. To have a mother seemed almost too good to be true. A mother who would be coming to see me! It never occurred to me to ask why I was not living with her. Why had I not seen her before for I could not remember seeing her? It was sufficient for me to know that she had been to see me and was coming again.

As I grew older I asked questions and Grandma gave me the kind of answers that suited her. It seemed that my father had had to go into hospital for the removal of a cyst in his chest. This was not thought to be malignant and therefore he would be coming home to recuperate and in time get back to his work. In the meantime he thought it might ease things a little for mother if one of us went away for a while. There were five of us. Two boys and three girls. I was the middle girl. The other two had serious problems with legs, eyes and health generally so I was the obvious choice. The boys, seven and five years old, went to day school, but while father was away mother had to look after the business which father had been painstakingly working up over a period of three years. He made and repaired baskets of all sizes and descriptions. Mother said he was so clever at it that he would only have to listen to the customer's request and know what the basket would be used for and he could be relied upon to come up with a first-time success. Sadly for all of us, father's plans did not work out as he would have wished.

I now had a mother but my life, day by day, did not change dramatically and school continued to be a mixed blessing. There, I had the company of other children, but rarely found any opportunity of becoming close to any one of them. They might carry over their friendships into their home lives. I was not allowed to bring children into the house, nor go outside to play with them. Grandma said, when I protested, 'You've got plenty of things to play with, so play with them!' Thus any relationships which I might have formed ended at the school gates. Occasionally we might visit a house where Grandma was acquainted with the parents of a child I knew, but even there I was not allowed out of sight or sound, which was frustrating and restrictive.

School day followed school day, sometimes interesting, sometimes monotonous, boring. Repetition of dull tables irritated me, I had no head for arithmetic. Getting to grips with pen and ink was another trial. Grandma complained on washing days that there must be more ink on my pinafore and dress than on the paper it was intended for. Our first introduction to proper writing was to copy from specially printed books. The first line contained pothooks, 'J'. Copying these taught us how to use the spaced lines which helped us to form our letters. Capitals took up two spaces, small letters one space — in depth, that is. Each letter had to be learned and properly formed before the linking-up process began. No matter how hard I tried, I never achieved the standard required by Teacher who wrote such beautiful copperplate on the blackboard. Eventually I came up with something which was decipherable and passed as writing.

I never achieved monitor status either. How nice it would have been to hear Teacher say, just once, 'Lucy Knowles, put out the inkwells,' or 'Collect the pens.' Most of my work fell far short of Teacher's idea of best. I did, however, get called out to read to the class. Once I was sent to the Headmistress to show her how well I had mastered this art. Such red-letter days were few and far between. Any attaching glory was always wiped away with the figures on my slate or exercise book when it came to arithmetic.

Of course, there were brighter times, for life can never be totally dull. Living on the borders of England and Wales had its compensations. My birthday is on May 24, known then as Empire Day, or the Queen's Birthday. I shared the date with Queen Victoria in whose reign the event had been a holiday. Schools still gave us a half holiday in remembrance. March 1 was St. David's day for Wales and that too was celebrated with a half holiday.

I liked singing lessons when we stood around Teacher's desk while she, with the magic of her tuning fork, set the note for us. We learned many old songs; some had been taught to successive generations of children. Traditional airs of Great Britain, England, Wales, Scotland and Ireland all provided us with songs. We sang the national anthems of England and Wales, also the one written for the thanksgiving service when the recovery of King Edward VII from a serious illness was celebrated: he was then the Prince of Wales. This song was a great favourite and it was quite a long time before I discovered that the third line of the chorus was, 'Let the prayer re-echo', and not, 'Let the prairies echo'. No one seemed to notice my mistake and I suppose it was just as suitable.

My education would certainly not have been complete without religious instruction. The first lesson each morning consisted of a prayer, a reading from the Bible and a hymn. Our teachers were of the Anglican persuasion and taught us from the Church of England Prayer Book. In addition to learning to recite passages from the Bible and the Psalms, we became proficient in the Creed, *Magnificat,* and the *Nunc Dimittis,* regardless of our baptismal state. It did no harm at all and probably laid good foundations in the children whose parents were of the un-Godly kind.

Chapter 7

Sunday was also Chapel day. I went to the morning service and to Sunday School in the afternoon. When I was very young I was put to bed after tea while Grandma went alone. I did not mind, and would lie in the great feather bed watching her getting ready to go out. I was quite fascinated by the way she secured her large hats by long hat-pins. I was convinced that they went right through her head and not just her hair. After Grandma had gone I listened to the lovely old church bells as they rang out the hymn tunes before the services. My favourite was *Through the Night of Doubt and Sorrow*. I knew it off by heart at an early age. Indeed I learned so many hymns and tunes that I am rarely at a loss to join in whenever I hear them played or sung. This always seems to surprise the young folk around me.

There were occasions when Grandma would not go to the morning service. I had to go alone and woe betide me if, when I reached home, I was not able to remember something that the preacher had said during his sermon. I had to know the text and which hymns were sung as well. Could this be how I developed a journalistic mind? Listening, observing and noting what went on around me. Collecting and storing away small items in my mind. Items to be brought out at some future date perhaps. Her intention would have been to keep my mind occupied so that I did nothing to distract other members of the congregation. It seems that I had a habit of counting the organ pipes, or turning the pages of my hymn-book noisily over when things appeared to be going too quietly. She could never have understood that here was the embryo of a writer in waiting.

Of course, singing played a great part in Chapel life. Every establishment had its choir or at least a lead singer. In our chapel, two elderly spinsters sat up in the gallery facing across to our seat. I watched spellbound at the way they opened their mouths. I could never hear the words but they appeared to be singing 'Blaw, Blaw' (as in 'raw'), mouths opening and closing like goldfish going after food. Joe Austin was quite a different kettle of fish. He sat behind us just under the brow of the main gallery. His deep resonant voice boomed out above all others. I used to turn around to watch him, the muscles in his throat and his Adam's apple competing with each other. He sang lustily and loud, but each word distinct and in perfect pitch. Grandma would give me a sharp nudge and whisper crossly, 'Turn around.' If I forgot and had another look it was, 'I've told you once. You wait till I get you home.' After that, of course, I had to be content with just listening, Grandma's wrath was something to be avoided at all costs.

Although we went to this particular chapel because it was nearest to us, there were times when Grandma liked to go somewhere else, or hear a visiting speaker for a change. This afforded us a better social life as we were always asked to attend the anniversaries, outings and Christmas parties. Preachers and deacons would try their hardest to try to persuade Grandma to become a full member of their chapel. She would have none of that, she preferred to 'be a free agent' and that is how she remained. Grandma had no time for the Anglican church, or the Roman Catholics. They had far too much ritual for her liking. 'All that dressing up!' she would snort. 'Jesus Christ didn't need all that finery to do his work, did he?' She may have been further prejudiced about the Roman Catholics because Grandpa, born in Cork, was surely baptised into that faith. Anything he did was wrong in her eyes, although he never attended any church or talked about religion except to say that, 'As long as there is a Pope in Rome there will be trouble in Ireland.' History alone may prove that one way or the other eventually.

Sunday School bored me. I must have played the poor teacher up although I don't remember much about it, except one time when I lay full length along one of the benches and announced that I was going to sleep. 'I wish you would, then we can all get on with the lesson,' that lady remarked. One afternoon she refused to let me into Sunday School at all. I remained outside the door until they all came out again and went off home as though nothing unusual had occurred. Grandma must never have heard about this event for I am sure I should have suffered for it. Although we did the rounds of all the chapels I went only to the one Sunday School. It was the practice that every child received a book at Christmas. One year, at the Christmas party and the gifts being handed out, it seemed that there was not one for me. Grandma spoke to the Superintendent about it: it was obviously an oversight. The man said that the rules had been changed and from now on only the regular attenders would be presented with a prize. They were having to cut down expenses in any case, but it was felt that better attendance would be forthcoming if the books were awarded on that basis. Grandma could not believe her ears, she drew herself up to her full height — which was not much anyway — and said quite firmly, 'Lucy will not be coming to Sunday School any more.'

I felt rather flattered to hear her sticking up for what she considered to be my rights. I was the more usual recipient of her caustic remarks. Although I was disappointed about the prize, I had no objection to leaving Sunday School, in fact, I was quite pleased. From then on I spent Sunday afternoons reading. I was permitted to read the Bible or Bible story books, rather a limited selection but at least I did not have to listen to a boring old woman lecturing me about Heaven.

Sometimes I went for a walk along the country lanes. There were no hidden perils then. Man and child could walk where they would without fear or harm. I was free until four o'clock when Grandma would have tea ready. Sunday teatime was slightly more interesting than week days; we had both jam and cake on the table on Sundays. Sewing and knitting were not allowed on Sunday. Housework was kept to a minimum. No cooking except for the breakfast porridge. Beds were not made, that is to say, the heavy mattresses were not turned but smoothed over and the sheets and blankets drawn up tidily. Under these rules it was easy for the housewife to attend her place of worship. No room for excuses on the grounds of 'too much to do'.

There were always books about the place. Grandma had evidently been quite a reader, but now, of course, I read to her. It gave her more time to get on with the mending or sewing some new clothes for me. She was very good with the needle, which was a blessing because she could not afford to have new things very often. Most of my coats and dresses were made from handouts from someone. The garment would be unpicked, the material well brushed and turned so that any fading on the topside could be hidden underneath.

If I read from the Bible she would do her best to explain its many mysteries to me, for, although I could read well, there were still many words that I did not understand. I read *Bleak House* by Dickens and a romantic novel *Annunciata* but I can't remember the name of the author. It was a thrilling story, where the man loses his lady love and everyone believes she is dead. Miraculously she lives and is restored to her lover. It made a deep impression on me, I had felt so upset for the hero at the death of Annunciata, and never quite understood how it came about that she was alive, but I was thrilled to tears when she finally turned up. Too long ago now for me to remember much about it.

When I was around nine years old a friend lent us a copy of the life story of John Williams, the missionary. The preacher at Chapel had often talked about his Calling, how God had called him to do His work. The further I read into the book the more engrossed I became, the more convinced that this was my calling. I would be a missionary. I would carry God's word to the furthermost ends of the earth. Beginning seriously to prepare myself, I held fervent meetings in readiness for the great crusade. I arranged my dolls along the sofa, Peter the cat came too, although he was just curious to see what was going on. There were carefully chosen Bible readings, hymns appropriate to the occasion, prayers, and, of course, a sermon. My pulpit was Grandma's armchair, and my perorations were given out over the back as I stood elevated there. Alas for my enthusiasm. On reaching the last chapter of the book I read of the great man's tragic death. Stepping from his boat on to some remote island shore John Williams was brutally clubbed to death by hostile natives. God went down in my estimation at that point. If He was really the Supreme Being, capable of ordering our lives, responsible for our welfare, how, oh how, could He allow this dreadful thing to happen? Preachers told you constantly, 'God is Love,' 'He will watch over you,' 'Pray unceasingly. God will answer your prayers.' Well, it seemed to me that prayer had not done much for poor John Williams. If a brave man like that could be so let down in his hour of need, what chance was there for the rest of us, poor miserable sinners?

Trying to envisage the sight, I thought those natives must have looked like the strange people pictured in some of Grandma's missionary books. They had bones through their noses, gashes down the sides of their faces and other modes of tortuous dress. They frightened me, I had never seen a coloured man. When I did, he was tall, good-looking and immaculately dressed. He was standing with some people looking down across the river to the racecourse beyond. I must have been staring at him. He leant down and said, 'Hello, little girl,' in the nicest voice. I fled as though all the devils in Hell were pursuing me. Grandma said, 'There's nothing to be afraid of. He is staying with Lady S—— for his summer vacation. He is at Oxford University, studying Law. He is a clever man.' Grandpa made one of his rare contributions to the conversation: 'That's right, bring 'em in, educate them, they'll overrun this country by the year 2,000.' That was in 1921.

Chapter 8

It was holiday time, and I was going to stay with my mother in Usk. Grandma walked with me across the meadow to the railway station, my spare clean clothes neatly packed into a small rush dress-basket. I wore my best serge dress and my Sunday button-up boots. All along Grandma kept up her ceaseless lecturing: 'Don't forget that I have brought you up to be a lady. See that you act like one. Please to show people that you know how to behave yourself. If you don't do as I say, mind I shall get to know and it will be the worse for you when you come home.' For once the tirade failed to irritate me. I just wanted the train to hurry up and come in so that I could get quickly away. Grandma went to the ticket window and bought my ticket, then went in search of a porter to enquire how long we might have to wait.

The great shiny monster thundered into the tiny station, its vibrant power making the ground tremble. The guard took care of my ticket but said he thought it would be nicer for me to travel in an empty carriage, rather than, as Grandma suggested, in his van. He promised to take good care of me. I was locked into the compartment, Grandma waved her hand, the guard waved his green flag and we were off. The train stopped twice; at each station the guard came along to see that I was alright before it started again. At a small country halt he unlocked the door and smiled up at me: 'The lights will be coming on soon because we are going through a tunnel. It will be a long one. Will you be afraid? Would you like to come into my van?' I declined his offer. 'Very well, then. I'll just lock your door again. You'll be alright. The next time we stop it will be yours.'

Off we went again and within a few minutes we were into the tunnel. I was prepared for the darkness, and the ceiling light had come on, but I was not prepared for the awful noise. It sounded to me as though giants were hurling huge rocks at the sides of the train, or banging them with sledge hammers. I had chosen to stay there alone, so I must put up with the situation. The whistle blew, the steam and smoke caught in the tunnel became lighter and at last we were out into the day-light. The train stopped, the door was unlocked and the guard helped me down from the carriage to the platform, remarking on what a very good traveller I had been. I heard shouts of, 'There she is!' and, 'There's our Lucy!' Two small figures came running forward to meet me; behind came a tall third figure. The first were my sisters, the other, my mother.

We laughed and chattered all the way home. Down under the railway bridge, along the main street, past all the shops. Someone on a doorstep said, 'I see you've got them all together. Aren't they like each other? Could be triplets.' Mother seemed very pleased about the things people said. She must have been so happy to have her three little girls all under her roof at the same time. It was the first time since being parted when father died. Melvina had come home for good from our aunt in Wales, Mary, of course, had never left mother, she had been a tiny baby when the home was broken up after our father died.

Lucy's mother, Annie Elizabeth Knowles, born 1880. Photograph taken c.1930.

The boys could not be with us but mother was working towards the day when we all would be together once again. It was so sad that when it actually happened she was dying with an inoperable cancer. Melvina and Mary took me on a tour of inspection around the house and garden, I was made to feel important. My opinion was called for on several matters: this was quite a new experience for me. I savoured it to the full. I had always been told I was stupid, a fool Grandma called me. Small wonder then that I fairly lapped up this new treatment like a cat laps cream.

Grandma's house was superbly furnished. She had very good taste and had filled her home with fine linen, good glass and china, also silver ware in abundance. All the rooms were well furnished and carpeted. She had scrimped and saved and worked for it, yet it had not brought her much happiness. In mother's home it was quite the reverse. Being for so long without a home while she worked for her stepmother, she had had to get together what she could, when she could, relying on sale rooms and markets for her furnishings. The necessities were there. A sturdy kitchen table, an odd assortment of chairs, cocomatting on the floor.

Being poor, said mother, was no excuse for being dirty or untidy. The whole house gleamed with what she laughingly called elbow-grease. She was such a resourceful soul, with every trick in the book at her disposal when it came down to brightening up the place. A spot of paraffin in the water made windows sparkle like crystal. A few drops of vinegar in the black-lead tin and the old iron fireplace came up like black silk. Bedroom and parlour floors were all given a good dose of Condy's Fluid — permanganate of potash to you — then polished for hours until they would have put shame to the floors in any mansion. Mother took in a little washing to help out the money and at nights, when folk were thinking of putting their feet up and taking things easy, she went off cheerfully to clean out some offices. She left home at eight o'clock but seldom got home before eleven o'clock.

Gas light had been laid on at the front part of the house but not at the back. When dusk came oil lamps were lit and hung on the walls of the kitchen. They cast a soft glow around, it glinted along brass candle sticks, they shone like gold and were further reflected in the old pictures that hung along the back wall. When the curtains had been drawn and the fire stirred up to a glowing blaze there was no better place on earth than that small room. We read books, played tiddley-winks, ludo or other games until bedtime, then cocoa and biscuits were lingered over. Cups and mugs came in odd assortment, you chose one and stayed with it until it got broken or something else pleased your eye better. Mother saw us up to bed before she went to work. We needed no candles, there was plenty of light from the street gas lamp which stood just outside our front door. We talked a while or sang or made up games in our heads until at last we fell tired but happily to sleep. Melvina and I shared a bed in the back room. Mary slept with mother in the front. Both rooms were really in the front of the house, but we named them back and front for convenience.

Some of the dolls I left at Grandma's were elegant creatures. Kid bodies and porcelain faces. Dressed in silks and satins and having hair that must not be combed, otherwise it all came away and left the poor thing quite bald. You had to always be sure to wash hands before playing with dolls like that. Here, at mother's, dolls were totally different. Huge homemade affairs with button eyes, darning-wool plaits, and stitched-in mouths. They all wore clothes which somebody's babies had outgrown. Indeed there was such a pile of clothing to choose from, including night attire, that you could pick something different each day if you wanted. The girls took one each to bed every night. I was not left out, to my joy. Loving hands had placed her ready at my side of the bed to await my arrival. I christened her Mollie. Mollie became a treasured possession and rarely left my side while I was there. I could not take her back to Grandma's. She would have banned such an object straight away. Poor Mollie might even have suffered the same kind of undignified end as dear old Charlie Chaplin. It had been arranged that I should now spend other school holidays with Mother, except for Christmas, so my dear Mollie waited patiently there for my subsequent return visits.

My mother had been most surprised to see me still in navy blue serge dresses, although I had a white embroidered frock for Sundays during the summer. As for my button-up boots they were dreadfully old-fashioned. Rummaging through her store of second-hand clothes donated by better-off relations, she found a couple of pretty dresses. There was a tussore silk, very popular at that time, and so easy to wash and iron. The other was blue gingham. With these two additions to my wardrobe I felt more like a lady every minute. A pair of black lace-up shoes were discovered, they fitted fine with tissue paper stuffed well down into the toes. To her joy Mother also came across a length of wide red satin ribbon. 'I'll iron that up,' she said. 'There's enough to make you each a sash for your Sunday frocks.' We trooped up the street hand in hand on Sunday afternoon resplendent in white starched frocks and red satin sashes tied in enormous bows at the back. People cast interested glances at us as we passed. We turned at the corner to wave to Mother who was still on the doorstep to watch us out of sight.

I felt grand and important going back to Grandma's at the end of the holiday and wearing the new clothes and the shoes. Grandma, however. was not at all pleased. I had been away for a month and in that time it seemed I had outgrown the hated boots. There was nothing she could do about it, there was no money to go out and buy new boots. She let her displeasure be known, verbally convincing as usual: 'Young ankles need supporting. There's going to be trouble later on wearing all these fancy shoes. You mark my words if I'm not proved right. Pandering to vanity it is.' I did not care. I had them!

Life seemed a bit flat and uninteresting after that glorious holiday, with a long garden to romp in, and a shady plum tree to sit under when the sun was too hot. I must have grown taller too, all the other clothes I possessed needed letting down or out. Clothes were made with plenty to spare in the hems, and tucks everywhere taking care of both height and girth. They had to grow with the wearer and save the unnecessary expense of buying new garments too often.

Chapter 9

When winter came I was always plagued with chilblains. I went around for months on end with plasters on my heels, and swollen fingers. Grandma told people that I was rather a delicate child. It might have been nearer the mark if she had said there was nothing wrong with me that could not have been put right with a good few solid meals on a regular basis. She was a firm believer in, 'Old is good', especially when it came to medicines or cures. Sore noses were liberally smeared with tallow candle fat. It smelt rancid and I went to bed nauseated on many occasions. My chest was treated to similar rubbings of camphorated oil, my back as well. I can well remember wearing a brown paper vest soaked in goose fat around my chest and back. It's a wonder I had any skin left on me after all these attempts at cold-curing. Sore throats were given a mixture of hot vinegar and honey. I hated it. Grandma said, 'Get on with it, drink it up, it's the nasty things that do us most good.'

In spite of, or perhaps because of, all these administrations, I still suffered a succession of coughs, colds and other ailments that seemed to me to be without end, a miserable outlook. I had whooping cough. Someone said that I had had scarlet fever, but I can't remember that. What I do most of all, and vividly, remember is the time I caught the measles. I awoke one morning unable to open my eyes. I suppose it could have been conjunctivitis, I was frightened. I shouted for Grandma. She came into the bedroom wanting to know what all the fuss was about: 'I can't see, I can't open my eyes.' If I was expecting sympathy I did not get it. 'It's God's punishment on you for being a naughty girl.'

She went downstairs to the kitchen. Now even more afraid than before, I searched around in my mind trying to think what terrible thing I must have done to incur the wrath of God. Unable to visualise myself facing the remainder of my days in utter darkness, yet convinced that God had struck me blind. It had been a cruel thing to say, but I don't suppose Grandma gave any thought to the effect such words might have on the mind of a child. After a while she returned, my glued-up eyelids were bathed in warm water and once again I was able to look around and see all the familiar objects. My relief was tremendous. Grandma said, 'You'd better stay in bed. I think you've got the measles. I'll have to fetch the doctor.' That did nothing to cheer me either. Our poor old doctor was a harsh man and shouted at everyone all the time. It was said that he'd been in the war and it had turned him against people.

For a while days seemed to merge into nights, and back again to days, with little happening except visits from the doctor, or the arrival at intervals of Grandma with warm drinks or medicine. She did not sit with me or read to me as I in later years have done with my own children when they were ill, and the hours in bed seemed long.

I awoke one afternoon to see my father sitting by my side. He was smiling at me, it did not seem strange that he should be there. His presence gave me a feeling of warmth as though I had just come out into the sunshine, although I knew the curtains were drawn across the windows because the doctor had said, 'Keep the light off her eyes.' We talked. I laughed, and he showed me how to make rabbits out of his hanky. What we said to each other I never could remember afterwards, it did not seem important to know. I only knew that I felt protected and safe. It must have been a bond of love, but I would not have understood about love at that time in my life. I mentioned Father's visit to Grandma. She did her best to convince me that it had all been a dream. She said, 'Forget it, go back to sleep.' I heard her telling a friend that I had been in a delirium, so I knew that I must have been very ill. Deliriums only happened to people who were very ill.

From the first few tottering steps between bed and chair I eventually regained my strength and better health. After this, life went on as before, that is until I had my tonsils out. The operation had become the fashionable thing to do at that time and was said to incur no risks to the young. Indeed it was thought to be beneficial in that, once the offending material was removed, there was much less chance of the patient getting colds or other infections. It turned out to be a never-forgotten and quite terrifying experience in my case. Also it added to my discomfort in ensuing years during which I suffered with chronic catarrh.

We walked to the hospital one summer morning. Grandma handed me over to a nurse, telling me that I was to be a good girl. I was, she said, only having my tonsils out and she would come back for me later on. The nurse, who was rather a severe-faced person, took me into a small barely-furnished room and left me. She returned after a while and undressed me, and put me into a long white nightgown, then secured my long hair very tightly within a white cap. No word passed between us and I was cold and fearful of my fate. Once again I was abandoned;

then a younger nurse came into the room and smiled but did not talk to me.

Having been told to be a good girl, and one of the golden rules being that I should never speak until I was spoken to, I dared not question the nurse. She sat down and took from her pocket a pair of small scissors. I wondered if she was going to use them to take out my tonsils. She trimmed her nails, then, popping the scissors back into her pocket, she picked me up and whisked me away through a dark corridor.

I have often since wondered why it had seemed so unnecessary to talk to a small child, give some comfort, or assurance that everything would be alright. In a state of terrified shock I was placed on a hard table, someone stuck a wedge in my mouth and placed an evil-smelling mask over my face. I tried to struggle free but strong hands held me firmly down. I know exactly how a defenceless animal feels when confronted with the horrors of vivisection. I dreamed that it was dark night. I was alone at the edge of a round pond. A golden moon rested on the far side but as I looked it started to circle the water. It came around with increasing swiftness. Each time it passed by me it emitted a sharp rasping sound which I felt vaguely must have something to do with me.

Whether the hospital administrators were as sparing in their use of chloroform as they seemed to be in lighting and conversation I don't know. All I know is that I reached consciousness while the offending tonsils were being drawn out of my mouth. Much to the annoyance of doctors and nurses I cried loud and long. Still crying hours later, I was fully dressed and lying on a couch at the end of a long ward. Sister was very cross with me, I was making far too much noise and it was disturbing her patients. One kindly man in a nearby bed said, 'Poor little thing. I daresay she's frightened.' To which the dragon replied sharply, 'I'm sure I don't know why, she's going home in a minute.' That was the first time I had heard home mentioned since I had arrived.

Grandma called for me with a child's open push-chair. Having walked to the hospital without difficulty that morning, I could not understand why I was now quite unable even to stand up unsupported. Grandma wrapped me up in her red flannel dressing gown and took me out. I secretly hoped we would not meet any of our acquaintances, especially school-mates, I felt so embarrassed in that thing.

That was also the year of the Peace celebrations. The horrid war now well behind us, the Town Council had decided to give a huge party for all the children of the town. It was set up on the Common one glorious summer day. Long trestle tables covered in snowy damask were piled high with sandwiches, cakes, buns, blancmanges, and jellies. There was lemonade and ginger-pop, or tea for those who preferred it. Swings were set up on the trees and organised games and competitions were arranged. The Mayor came along to present each child with a Peace mug and a bag of sweets.

That's what the girls at school told me when I questioned them. I never did care much for the crowded scene and sought the seclusion of a nearby garden. I was just going to play there for a little while, then go on to the party in time for the tea. Alas, the day was warm, the air in the garden sweetly fragrant. I fell asleep! When I awoke and climbed back over the wall on to the Common, women were clearing away the tables. The party-goers had left. There on a table lay a solitary mug and a bag of sweets. Two ladies hovered. One said rather sharply, 'Where have you been?' I truthfully replied, 'I couldn't come before.' 'Well,' said the other lady, 'you're here now, you'd better have these.' She handed over the mug and the sweets, then, as an afterthought, she dived down into one of the cardboard boxes and brought out a Chelsea bun. 'You might as well have this too,' she said. I took it gratefully. I was hungry and knew that there would be no tea awaiting me when I arrived home. The other lady did not look at all pleased but I saw her point. It's not really the thing to turn up expecting gifts after the party is over.

I took my presents home to Grandma. She let me eat the bun but the sweets were put to one side to be doled out in intervals over the week. The mug found a home on the top shelf of the what-not among the other decorative but useless items. It was crowded with pieces of celebratory ware from past occasions. I hoped that Grandma would not start asking awkward questions about the party or that someone would not tell her of my escapade. It obviously never occurred to her that I had been anywhere but at the Peace Party, and life went on as before.

Sleeping in the great feather bed in Grandma's room I woke up one night to see her preparing for bed. Sitting up I said, 'Grandma, Lily Davies is dead!' She looked at me in a bemused way, as she sometimes did when she was not quite sure whether to believe what I was saying. 'Oh, go to sleep, you've been dreaming.' The matter was too important to be dropped like that. 'She is, Grandma, she is dead. I heard the bell ringing for her.' It was the custom to toll the church bell when a funeral was about to take place, but, of course, I could not have heard it at that late hour. Yet the information was clear in my mind and had to be told. I repeated it. Grandma got cross. 'Turn over and go to sleep and don't talk such rubbish,' she said sharply. The very next day we heard that Lily had died at ten o'clock the previous night, a victim to scarlet fever. She was five-years-old.

There were other times when I confounded Grandma with my pre-knowledge of things which happened. This perceptive power faded as I became older and more involved with worldly matters.

Chapter 10

During the late spring and summer months, often right through autumn, we went for long walks in the country after an early tea. There were so many pretty places to see not too far away for small legs to deal with. From these walks I became gradually aware of Nature's beauty. The wonder of a perfectly formed flower, a delicate bud, the sweet song of a bird, a brilliant sunset. Roads were very quiet then, very few people had a car or motorbike and, although buses were beginning to replace the high-seated draughty charabancs, they were still few and far between. Sometimes, if Grandma did not feel like a long walk, we might visit a friend. Three I remember in particular, although, of course, there were many, also distant relatives on Grandma's side of the family who followed her father's trade and took care of all the boot making and repairing around the district.

Mrs. Deacon was married to a man much older than herself. He was rotund, jolly, always telling jokes or riddles and usually laughing. She was tall and slender, and dressed her hair after the style of Queen Alexandra with a fringe on the forehead. The clothes she wore were not at all in keeping with her station in life, Grandma said. Most women went about in dark clothes, but Mrs. Deacon wore gowns of pastel shades, silks and satins, some richly embroidered with gold or silver thread. I suppose such apparel would not have been out of place in a dance hall or ballroom. Although Grandma scoffed, I quite liked the light colours, they certainly cheered things up a bit, and made her look quite handsome. 'Handsome is as handsome does,' was Grandma's broadside on that.

The Deacons' house was so full of furniture that it was difficult to move around. It was Mrs.Deacon's second marriage and she had brought the contents of her former home with her to her new husband's already well-stocked home. It was a funny old building, three storeys high, but only the width of one room, with narrow passages for access. There were two rooms on each floor, one behind the other, except for the top floor which was one long room with a window at each end. The front room downstairs was Mr. Deacon's office, although I never discovered the nature of his business. In the evenings he always put on a velvet jacket and an embroidered smoking cap before settling down in his old armchair in the living room. There he would smoke his pipe to his heart's content and listen to his young wife as she regaled him with the items of news or gossip. He would listen and chuckle away until at last he would break out into roars of full-bellied laughter. He always seemed to be such a happy man.

Each year on the anniversary of her first husband's death, Mrs. Deacon made a pilgrimage to his grave. She set off armed with buckets and soap and cloths and scrubbing brush. Once arrived at the cemetery, she begged hot water at the sexton's lodge and went to work on the grave. She scrubbed the marble headstone and the matching surrounds, and when they were dry they were treated to a good polish, just to preserve them from the elements, she said. All the tiny chippings of marble which filled in the centre of the plot were gathered up into her empty buckets and carried home. There they were put into hot soda water and left until the next day, when they too would be scrubbed over and dried. After all this Mrs. Deacon returned them to their rightful resting place.

I sometimes went up to the top floor of the house with Mrs. Deacon if she was busy baking. She kept all her baking equipment up there, also her clothes press, mangle and flat irons. Goodness knows why, for all the actual cooking and the washing had to be done down on the ground floor. Perhaps it was her escape from the overcrowded lower regions where there were two of everything, including huge dark oak sideboards which took up the whole of one side of the living room. When her work was finished she would throw up the window sash in the front top room and look out on the narrow street below, watching the people as they passed beneath. She certainly had room to breathe up there, it was light and airy.

Mr. and Mrs. Eldon were great travellers. Although somewhat staid and old-fashioned in their views, they dressed well and made the long crossing to America every other year to visit their daughter and grandchildren. Mrs. Eldon was American by birth, Mr.Eldon, now retired, came from a good English family and had at one time held some kind of diplomatic post over there, where he met and married his wife. Mrs. Eldon's hair was quite magnificent. She was an old woman, over 70, yet her hair was rich auburn and plentiful. She dressed it stylishly to form a halo around her head. Her hobby was making pillow lace and I often stood beside her, spellbound, fascinated at the way her still nimble fingers manipulated the bobbins, weaving them over and under to form exquisite patterns in lace from the finest of fine cotton.

The house was large, square, and stood in a neat plot close by the river. The whole place was a veritable Aladdin's Cave. Anyone possessing a quarter of its treasures would at today's values be a wealthy person. I often wonder about all the fine *objet d'art* items that were even then being thrown on scrap heaps in order to keep up with the *nouveau riche* modern trends of that period. Mantlepieces were weighed down with bronze figurines, donkeys with nodding heads, knights clad in full armour astride splendid steeds and Chinese mandarins who bowed to you at the lightest touch of a finger.

Mr. Eldon had a smooth-haired terrier, a very friendly animal who allowed me to accompany him on walks around the garden. Mrs. Eldon's pet was quite a different matter, a spoilt vicious pedigree Chinese Pekinese. I kept well away from his spiteful teeth. It made an afternoon distraction for me on Saturdays. I was usually hospitably received at the front door. Mrs. Eldon never said much to me but Mr.Eldon always seemed pleased to have my company and would tell me many interesting things which I have long since forgotten.

One Saturday Grandma gave me a letter to take down in the morning. I knocked on the door for a long time without getting any response. I made my way around to the back of the house, the tradesmen's entrance, and knocked and hammered there for ages. At last a very cross voice demanded to know what I wanted, but the door was not opened to me. I could not put the letter through the letter box because Grandma had strictly told me to hand it to Mrs. Eldon in person. Mrs. Eldon was deaf so it was difficult trying to explain the situation. Her high-pitched voice came at me through the closed door: 'You can't come in now, go away, I never see people in the morning.'

Eventually, she realised who I was and unbolted the door, just opening it sufficiently for me to hand over the message. After another long wait — on the doorstep — Mrs. Eldon came back and handed me her written reply, quickly shut the door again and I heard the bolts being pushed into place. The fleeting glimpse I had of her through the narrow door opening revealed a different Mrs. Eldon to that one I was used to seeing. She had a long dark gown on and her head was tightly swathed in a white silk scarf. So closely was it bound that the contours of her skull were such that she seemed to have no hair at all.

I told Grandma how I had been kept waiting and how cross Mrs. Eldon had been. Not the kind of reception I was used to, when I would be graciously treated to a glass of homemade lemonade and a biscuit. Then I was allowed to sit on a beaded foot stool and enjoy the hospitality. When I mentioned the headscarf and the strange sight I had seen, Grandma merely smiled mysteriously and said, 'Yes, well —.' I think now that she had purposely sent me down there on the Saturday morning especially to find out whether Mrs. Eldon wore a wig. Obviously she did! The matter would probably be a subject for discussion when Grandma's friend came to call. I often heard things about people which I am quite sure I was never intended to know.

Mrs. Mason was a much nicer person. She was over 80 years of age when I knew her. All her clothes were black, even her aprons, and around her neck she wore several strands of jet beads. She was a short dumpy little woman, very like the old Queen Victoria, and like Victoria she always wore a little lace cap. Weekday caps were trimmed with black ribbon, on Sundays the bow would be purple. I decided that when I grew old like Mrs. Mason I too would wear a little lace cap for it seemed to me to be the very height of ladylikeness and elegance.

The house was little more than a cottage but crammed with Victoriana. You walked straight in from the street into the living room but Mrs. Mason had made it more private by making a passageway with two large screens, thus hiding from view the interior. The screens were a source of great interest to me because they were decorated in a fashion that was then beginning to go out with pictures cut from magazines and other cut-outs of birds and animals or flowers which could be bought especially for that purpose for a few coppers. These were pasted over the entire area of the screens. I studied them each time I went there and usually managed to find some that had previously eluded me.

In the narrow passageway there was a large well-polished chest of drawers. On top of this stood many things to be looked at. Stuffed birds, and a tiny stag in genuine hide and complete with a set of miniature antlers. It stood about six inches high and was encased in a glass dome. There was, too, a tiny white china chest of drawers with what I imagined then to be pure gold knobs. This too was under a dome. I secretly hoped that Mrs. Mason would notice the interest I always showed in this particular piece. Perhaps one day she would give it to me. The main object, the centre piece of the collection, was one of those artificial lily wreaths that people used to put on graves. They were encased in a glass cover and took the place of fresh flowers in cases where it was not possible to make regular visits to the cemetery.

Mrs. Mason had grown too old to visit even occasionally, and had brought the wreath home in its casing from her husband's grave so that she could look after it and keep it safe and clean. Her husband had died shortly after they had been married. When speaking to anyone she often brought his name into the conversation, almost as though she expected him to be coming through the door at any minute. Perhaps it was because she was so old, her love had been deep and true, she must have thought about him constantly although he had been dead for at least 60 years. She would say things like, 'Paul says —', or, 'Oh, Paul would not like that.'

Her sole companion was the grey and red African parrot that Paul had bought for her as a wedding gift. The intelligent old bird knew all the tradesmen. When his mistress was upstairs or in the yard he would whistle shrilly or croak raspingly to tell her who had called. He knew the calls of the baker and the milkman and could imitate their 'Milko's' and 'Fresh bread today'. He was as good as a watch dog any day but could be a nuisance at mealtimes. He would put his head to one side and say, 'Polly want, Polly want, oh, poor Polly!' He'd keep it up until you pushed a little of whatever was on your plate through the bars of his cage; then he would settle down quietly again.

I often went to Mrs. Mason's on Saturdays, her eyesight was failing and I did errands for her. She also liked me to read to her. She had many books and must have been an avid reader during her lifetime. After a reading session she sometimes took me out to the 'apple room'. This was just a lean-to but sound attachment to the end of the house. Here she stored the large juicy Blenheim apples from her trees at the bottom of the garden. They were looked over regularly and turned, any that needed using quickly were taken out then. Mrs.Mason usually gave me two, one to eat there and one to take home.

There were many intriguing things to look at in that house. There was the fly trap, which was kept half-filled with water into which the unsuspecting flies found their way but from which they were quite unable to escape. When wasps were about Mrs. Mason would put a little bit of jam into the water to attract them; she did not like the sticky fly papers which most other people hung from their ceilings. Of course, in those days you were plagued with flies during the summer months, especially if you lived near the river where there was usually a greater variety, but all with the same purpose, to annoy you with their buzzing and do their best to destroy your food. It was constant war.

The most fantastic thing of all in Mrs. Mason's was the upstairs lavatory. Grandma and I went there once when the old lady was ill in bed. Curtains hung down around the bedhead and a little frill ran around the brass rail which at one time would have held curtains to enclose the occupant of the four-poster and keep out the draught. Beside the bed was a magnificent carved mahogany chair that looked for all the world like a throne. Within its seated depths lay a porcelain lavatory pan decorated with blue flowers. It was a flush toilet and the cistern overhead was encased in mahogany. Armrests were stout and beautifully carved, and when not in use the lid was closed over and covered with a cushion. I had thought that we were well off in having an indoor flush toilet when most people had to trudge up the garden path in all weathers to satisfy their needs. But this to my mind was the height of luxury, and to be honest I have only ever seen one other such arrangement — and that in a stately home somewhere.

What I liked about Mrs.Mason was that she never talked down to me. Unlike other people she treated me as an equal and accepted me as a friend. She was always most grateful for any little thing I was able to do to help her. I would like to think that she was re-united with her beloved Paul when she journeyed out into the after-life.

Chapter 11

My contribution to the upkeep of the household came on Saturday morning directly after breakfast. This consisted of polishing the brasses, picking up the bits, and cleaning the knives. There was a sense of achievement in cleaning the brass door knobs and the front-door letter-box, and I did not really mind the boring job of crawling around the bedroom floors picking up little bits of fluff or cotton which had found their way there from the feather beds and blankets.

What I absolutely hated was cleaning the knives. It was before the advent of stainless steel, and knives used once turned colour, and, if you had had any food with vinegar in it, the blades left a nasty taste when you were eating potatoes or other vegetables that seemed to pick up the unpleasant flavour. Larger households than ours would, of course, have their knives cleaned each day. Some people had machines into which you inserted the blades of the knives, then, by turning a handle, buffing pads inside the contraption took away the stains for you without too much effort. Grandma decided that it was a waste of time doing our few every day so it became a once-a-week chore. Out would come the board: this was about fourteen-inches long and the width of a table knife. Yellow brick-dust was sprinkled on it, then the knives must be drawn back and forth along the leather-topped board or rubbed in a circular motion until all the stains were removed. How my arms ached as I drew the blades across the powdered board. I changed hands to relieve the strain but it was always a painful exercise. Grandma always inspected the work closely. If it was not up to her standard then you had to do it all over again, so you just had to stick to it and be glad that the job was only done once each week.

Grandma always believed that Satan found work for idle hands and she made sure that I should be well-occupied, using the day to good purpose. When cold winter brought the long dark evenings she would gather together all the mending. I learned to sew quite early in life. My apprenticeship began with unpicking. Seams in old coats were unpicked, the cloth turned and made up into other garments suitable for school. There was no sewing machine, it was all done by sheer slog. But the end result was good, and eventually the smell of long storage in moth balls would evaporate and I would have a winter coat or dress, or Grandma a new skirt. Worn sheets would be cut down the middle and turned sides to middle and I laboriously worked my way down endless seams and edges that went on for ever.

The work was usually done by candle light, for, although gas was laid on, Grandma had for long practised the art of thrift and did not consider that it was necessary to burn gas when candles would do just as well and were, of course, cheaper. Sometimes we even did these jobs by firelight. I often read by this as well, for when the coals stirred up they gave out bright golden flames. The quality of coal seems to me to have greatly deteriorated since those days. I read anything and everything, from the labels on food packets to great books from the shelf, but not always with understanding.

One evening a friend called to see Grandma. They had quite a conversation going when I decided with my superior knowledge to put in my spoke: 'Mr. Bell, our milkman, has gone to prison.' They stopped talking. I went on: 'He committed adultery.' The sudden thick silence was broken as Grandma said, 'What do you mean?' She had rather an odd look on her face. I revealed all: 'You know, Grandma, it was in the paper. He put water into the milk.' I never understood why they laughed so much. Tears ran down their faces. I saw nothing to laugh about, it had all been there in the local newspaper for everyone to read. The commandment in the Bible said quite clearly: 'Thou shalt not commit adultery.' The visitor said, 'Out of the mouths of babes and sucklings.' Grandma parried, 'Where ignorance is bliss 'tis folly to be wise.' I did not understand that either, but it seemed that old folk were very fond of quoting things they had read. After a while I learned more about adultery and adulteration. It was a grave offence for milkmen to add water to the milk; they went to prison unless they were able to pay a heavy fine.

The highlight of winter was, of course, Christmas, and school teachers arranged parties for the children on the last day of term. These were strictly-organised functions, no romping around. Tea was under the supervision of the Headmistress. No one got away with anything until they had eaten at least two of the great doorstep wedges of bread and butter. Jellies were donated by loving mums who also did some of the baking. After tea there was usually a school show-off to get up on a table and give a monologue or a long poem. Indoor games like musical chairs and oranges and lemons came next and the grand finale was the presentation of gifts. Gifts were the free samples and games from well-known firms or industries. Teachers wrote off each year for all these items and I think it became a contest between them to see which teacher obtained the larger variety. We had toothpaste, boot polish, cocoa, advertising matter in the form of general knowledge booklets, games, painting sets, crayons and picture books. We went home, our arms loaded with treasure.

I was a bit confused about Christmas. Children at school kept on talking about Santa Claus, the mysterious old gentleman in a red suit who came down the chimney on Christmas Eve to leave gifts for boys and girls who had been good. I remember once when I was very young seeing Grandma pinning one of my school socks to the mantlepiece for this visitor to fill. It only happened once and I cannot remember what was put into my sock, if anything. After that Grandma said it was all a lot of rubbish. Christmas for me was a down-to-earth affair. Grandpa never showed up at Christmas; he preferred being with his friends, 'cronies' Grandma called them. She usually had some disparaging things to say about him, but I knew that, had he stayed at home, he would not have been welcomed and probably would have spent most of the time upstairs in his little room. I never saw him sit by the fire as other men do. He sat on the chair nearest to the door when he came in for meals, and made a quick get-away as soon as he had finished.

Just before Christmas the house had to be thoroughly 'gone over', everything was to be sparkling bright. Holly and mistletoe adorned pictures and mirrors, giving a festive air. Fresh fruit appeared on the sideboard and a bottle of ginger wine was put in the cupboard ready for the great day.

On the Eve I was bathed regardless of whether it was regular bath night or not. My hair was washed and screwed up uncomfortably tight in order to bring to it some semblance of curl, for God had seen fit to bestow poker-straight locks to me. The knots were tight against my skin and it was difficult to find a painless resting position.

On Christmas morning I had to stay upstairs until I was called down to breakfast. The meal, porridge or fried bread, would be eaten in silence while Grandma went off to the back kitchen where lay the ancient coal range which came into its own on such occasions. It was of a vintage style but served us well and kept the steam from pudding-boiling and the smell of roast away from the living room. As I ate my breakfast my gaze would surreptitiously fall upon the big armchair beneath the window. It would be covered over with a large thick table-cloth or curtain. The shape was intriguing with its lumps and bumps. But I dared not get down from the table to have a sly look in case Grandma came in and caught me. She usually knew or found out very quickly if I got up to anything I should not be doing.

Once the table had been cleared, however, the cover was whipped off to reveal a pile of brown paper parcels. All were addressed to me. How the postman had been able to deliver all those without me knowing I never discovered. Grandma must have had a good hiding place, too, because I had free access to all cupboards and I never came across anything. I had many aunts and uncles who, although they had their own large families to provide for, always found time to send something to a lonely little girl on birthdays and at Christmas.

It usually took some time for me to discover the contents of parcels, string must never be cut, that was just wasteful. However tight the knots, and some were sealed with wax, they must be fiddled with and eased out until they could be untied and the string rolled into neat little

43

balls for use later on. Paper wrappings were carefully undone and smoothed out and folded, put away for future use. Nothing was ever wasted. Only then could I begin to savour the delights of the operation. There would be board games, toys and, best of all, books. Many beautiful annuals came my way and I treasured them for years.

Christmas dinner was an elaborate affair. Although there were only the two of us, Grandma liked to do things properly. The dining table was extended and spread with the best damask cloth and matching napkins, laid with the cutlery — cleaned by me the previous day — and flanked by sparkling glass. Brightly coloured crackers and small sprigs of berried holly were used for decoration. We ate our chicken and roasted potatoes with greens and bread sauce off the best Royal Doulton service, brought out of its display cabinet only on very special occasions. Christmas pudding followed, served with sweet white sauce. The shiny silver threepenny-bit that had been pushed into the pudding at some stage always found its way on to my plate. Mince pies, hot from the oven, and perhaps an orange, if we could find room for it, came next, rounded off with a glass of ginger wine. It was indeed a banquet. When the normal tea-time hour arrived we only craved a cup of tea and a slice of cake. By this time I had been able to really get down to enjoying my gifts, leafing through the books as a foretaste of pleasures to come. Grandma had a nap after all that. I was allowed to stay up for at least an hour past the usual bedtime, while we regaled ourselves further with nuts or fruit. Christmas was a grand time, a luxurious time!

On Boxing Day we came back down to earth. The toy cupboard had to be cleared out and room made for the new things. Sadly, it often meant parting with a favourite, but if glue or needle and thread could not mend it, then it was the fire or the dustcart. The more presents you received the more letters to write. It was done without complaint, it was the right thing to do, people expected no less of you.

Grandma stood by to tell me what to write and to make sure I knew how to set a letter out. Room had to be left too for her to add a few words at the end. I liked doing letters, learning how to begin and how to end. My difficulty these days is not how to begin, or end, but when to stop!

Chapter 12

The time had come for me to move on, to leave the Mixed Infants' friendly little school around the corner. Boys and girls must now be segregated, boys to the school in the town centre and girls henceforth to an ancient building on the town boundary. If they were brainy, of course, they might get into the Girls' High School, that enormous imposing pile that sat on a hill.

I now had a long walk, twice there and twice back again each day. It was quite pleasant in summer but awful in the winter. Some children who lived outside the town or in outlying farms had great difficulty. For them it could mean a walk of three miles each way. In the winter they brought sandwiches, and the Headmistress let them sit in the classroom to eat them. If the weather was very cold she would make mugs of hot cocoa for them but otherwise their drinks were from the tap in the yard. Sometimes their fathers would fetch them at teatime in the farm carts because often the roads were icy or, where the roads were very low, floods were a hazard. During the winter term dinner hour was shortened so that the children might at least set off home in daylight. This caused problems for me. Grandma did not hold with all that messing about with times. She refused to make dinner earlier and consequently I arrived late at school every afternoon and got caned for it.

Long before my time Grandma had fallen out with the teachers who

Monnow Bridge, Monmouth, in July 1907. The gate tower on this bridge was erected late in the 13th century as a defensive work and toll gate for the western approach to the town.

45

had also taught my aunts when they attended the school. Teachers never seemed to retire in those days, most of them were grey, if not white-haired, and had little patience. Grandma called them all 'brazen hussies' and the feud went on, although I very much doubt if they even remembered what the fuss had been about in the beginning.

Talk about Dickensian treatment! They should have lived in the great writer's time. They certainly came up to his impressions of people who had to deal with the young. They took it out of me, whether I was the culprit or not. I was often punished for the smallest misdemeanour by having to sit out under the bell tower. This was not a happy place to be in winter when the rain seeped in and you had been given a copy of the Bible to read. They found the one with the smallest print and, if you've never seen some of those ancient Bibles, you will not be able to understand how very tiny the printing was. I do not know how the type setters managed to get them set out, it must have been a great strain on their eyes. It was a strain on mine trying to read them. I was told repeatedly that I was a fool, and I even remember one teacher banging my head against the wall. It is a wonder that I did not end up being a complete idiot. I learnt very little at that school. I was so often outside the classroom doing penance for something or another, or my eyes were too dimmed by tears to see the blackboard clearly.

In the early summer of my second year there I caught impetigo, a highly infectious and very unpleasant skin complaint. This meant staying away from school on doctor's orders for six weeks. The end of this period coincided with the commencement of the summer holidays so I did not get back to school until the autumn term began. Everyone automatically 'went up' after the summer — but not me! All the explanations were brushed aside and, unavoidable as it had been, my prolonged absence was given as the reason for my being kept down. This meant another year doing the same lessons, but with the younger girls. I was both hurt and humiliated.

Morning brought prayers, Bible readings, or psalms and hymns. They are forever engraved on my mind. *Praise to the Holiest in the Heights* and *Lead Kindly Light*. I never felt much like praising and the 'light' of knowledge I longed for was denied me.

That was the way it went until I was nearing my eleventh birthday. Suddenly, almost overnight, everything changed. I had noticed that Grandma had been doing an unusual amount of washing and sorting out of the household linen, also cupboards and drawers, undisturbed for years, were being turned out and not refilled. Some large pieces of furniture disappeared, to the sale room I was told. No further explanations came my way and I did not care to ask too many questions. Questions were generally frowned upon if connected with household matters.

One Friday morning Grandma said, just as I was going off to school, 'Tell the teacher that you will not be there on Monday. We are going away.' Before I could reply she continued as if expecting me to ask, 'Never mind where. I don't want those nosy teachers to know my business. If I don't tell you, you can't tell them.' I always kept as much distance between myself and teachers as possible, and did not get around to telling them the news. I did not think it mattered, perhaps it might even be better to keep it back until leaving at four o'clock. At dinner time Grandma had other ideas. 'You needn't go back to school this afternoon. I can do with you here. There are things you can do.'

So there it was, they never got the message. I was very relieved at not having to go there any more, yet at the same time consumed with curiosity as to what went on when I failed to put in an appearance on the following Monday morning. Were they perhaps getting ready to chastise me for not being there on Friday? Oh, what would they say when they found out that I had left for ever without so much as a goodbye?

The move must have been planned for and arranged long before I knew. Grandma in her Victorian ways did not believe in telling children anything until it was absolutely necessary. By the time Saturday night came there was little left to do in the way of packing. All the carpets had been rolled up and were standing in the hall. Tea chests were full of silver, glass and china, while clothes and linen goods had been tightly pressed into huge leather trunks and secured with heavy leather straps. Although the place was in such a state of upheaval, Grandma did not intend to become Godless overnight. Sunday was observed in the usual way. It was the Lord's Day, we went to Chapel, as if nothing had happened, or was to happen.

Monday morning we were up very early. I was going to travel by train with Grandpa to South Wales. The secret was out. Grandma was to stay behind and would travel with the driver to ensure the safe handling of all our goods and chattels. Peter, the cat, was already protesting loudly from within his temporary prison, the cat basket.

I should have liked to have stayed behind too, I felt I was missing a lot of interesting events. However, there was some compensation in the knowledge that Grandpa and I were going to the station by cab. This was the first stage of our journey into the unknown, the nearest thing to an adventure that I had ever known. Grandpa stood in the hall leaning on his stick, his last remaining black suit and his best bowler hat well brushed. Both had seen too many better days to look smart. The cab arrived, it was the only one remaining in the town but much favoured by the older folk who did not care for the newfangled contraptions that were beginning to take over the streets: they preferred the unhurried steady horse-driven vehicle. Mr. Pierce was an old man, tall, gaunt. He wore a grey cap and a long heavy overcoat which he wrapped about his legs, for he sat outside the coach, perched up on high above the horse. He knew his place in the scheme of life and never treated his clients with anything but the greatest of courtesy.

The cab was dark inside and smelt of soap and leather. The windows which formed the top half of the doors could be let down on a strap on warm days, like the railway carriage windows. There was plenty of room for Grandpa and me inside with our few necessary belongings. We went out of our front door, down the steps for ever. I see the house now in my mind's eye, my first remembered home.

Chapter 13

The journey into Wales — we were going into the Rhondda Valley — was not really very long, but it took a long time because we had to change trains and wait a full hour between the first and second half of the journey. Time spent sitting on the platform waiting for our connection was wiled away by Grandpa's stories. He had little opportunity of any conversation with me at home so perhaps he felt he ought to take full advantage of the spare time. He must have been a lonely old man, and probably sensed the loneliness in me too.

I had never thought that there could be any danger in rail travel and the possibility of a train crash had never entered my head. But then Grandpa began his stories and finished up with instructions on what to do in the event of such an occurrence: 'When you feel the impact coming, kneel upon the seat with your back outwards, press your face into the upholstery and hold your hands firmly above your head, keeping your face covered at all times.' This procedure, he said, would most probably save my life and at any rate would considerably lessen any injuries I might sustain. For many a night after that I went to bed and sweated in fear as I went over the instructions. The most worrying thing was, how would you know that a crash was coming? I have since wondered whether he had been involved in a disaster. He was very old, over 80 years of age when we went to Wales, and there had been a train crash in Ireland during the nineteenth century.

Arriving at last at our final destination, Treorchy, we were met by a young woman who introduced herself to us as my cousin Ivy. I had never heard of her before this, but she was very friendly and carried Grandpa's case for him as we walked to Cwmparc. It was hot and sunny and several times he had to stop to get his breath while going up the steep hilly road. We were not used to hills. Our old home had been a flat place, hills were outside the town and only used for outings or long walks for the young and the energetic. We were both relieved when cousin Ivy said, 'Here we are. In you go, Grandpa,' and let us into a house with a long dark passage. We came out into a room lit with sunshine and met my Aunt Lily. She was a buxom motherly kind of person, dressed in grey with a snowy white apron and a lovely smile. Grandpa was quickly settled in a large armchair near the fire. I discovered that everyone in Wales always kept a roaring fire going all the time, even in summer. How else could they have baked all the pies and cakes that Welsh people delighted in making, or provided the constant hot water for men's baths and washing? There were no pit-head baths in those days.

Aunt Lily set a meal of boiled eggs, well-buttered homemade bread and gooseberry pie with custard. After that we had a cup of tea and biscuits. Aunt said kindly, 'Grandad must be very tired, poor old gentleman. Let him have a little nap now.' To me, she said, as she rummaged in the bottom of a cupboard, 'Here you are,' and handed me a ball and a skipping rope. 'Go out the back and play now. I'll call you in when the girls come home from school.' She didn't explain who 'the girls' were but I later found out that they were two more cousins, younger sisters of Ivy, and Georgina whom we had not yet met; she had gone off visiting somewhere. Myra was 13 and Esther 11 like me. They introduced me to their father who was shut away in a hut at the bottom of the garden. Uncle Henry was a very quiet man who rarely spoke unless spoken to. Perhaps he was a bit overwhelmed with women, having five of them in his household. He was one of Grandpa's many sons.

Henry spent his days among his tools and piles of boots and shoes, many of which looked past redemption, yet his skills could be relied upon to extract yet another few months' wear from them. He had inherited the skills of his grandfather, a grandfather who had taught his sons well. All around the country there were shoe repairers bearing his name. His eldest son had gone off to Weymouth and established a high-class boot and shoe shop. Grandma was very proud of him and would tell people about his success. It was said that when this son left home his mother — my great-grandmother — had cried and said her, 'Jem had gone to foreign parts.' To leave home and move into the next town was an event in those days, but to go right away to the unknown southern part of England was akin to transportation in her eyes. She believed that she would never see him again.

Aunt called us in to tea. Cold boiled ham, lettuce crisp and fresh from the garden, and homemade bread, jam, pickles, custard pie and treacle tart. Welsh cakes as well. What a feast! I had never seen so much food on a table in my life. I thought Aunt and Uncle must be very rich to be able to put on such a sumptuous meal. Grandpa looked rested and joined in the talk about many things, including his state of health.

When the tea was over Aunt said, 'Myra and Esther will take you home now. I expect Grandma is waiting for you. Grandad is going to stay here for a few days, we've plenty of room.' Grandpa fairly lapped up the treatment, the adulation bestowed upon him. Aunt obviously thought he was a wonderful old man and made her feelings about Grandma abundantly clear. 'Wicked old woman,' she said. 'The way she treats your poor grandad, shameful.' This was the first time I had heard anyone express such remarks about Grandma, I began to see her in a different light. All the same, I kept my thoughts to myself.

The girls took me down the hill, past the school, the one I should be going to, Esther said. I was not particularly pleased about that and hoped that the evil day might be put off as long as possible. Esther was pleased, though. 'We'll be in the same class,' she said. It was the last place on earth that I wanted to be. At the end of the street we turned off into a little road with ten houses — five a side — with a shallow river flowing across the end. 'That's your house': Myra pointed to the last house on the right-hand side of Clare Road. It had a long garden running down to the river's edge.

Myra knocked on the door, which after a minute was opened by Grandma. We went inside. Everything was piled up all over the place. It was utter chaos. I had never seen anything like it and stood there bemused, wondering how it could all come straight, and if it didn't how would we live in it. I felt that the girls would have liked to have stayed but Grandma sent them away almost as soon as we arrived. 'Thank you for bringing Lucy home. You'd better go now, come and see us when the place is tidy.' They went and I began to wander around the packing cases. I was looking for Peter whose pitiful cries could be heard as he bemoaned his fate.

Grandma had lit a fire. 'Come through here and make yourself useful,' she said, pointing to a large basket. 'The little teapot and some cups are in there. Get them out and I'll make a cup of tea.' The kettle was already singing and soon we were having tea and biscuits, that was all there was to eat until tomorrow. 'Can I let Peter out?' I asked. 'I'll lock all to doors first', Grandma replied. 'We must not let him get outside or we shall lose him.' I protested on account of his probably needing to see to his toilet. 'Shut him in the back kitchen, we'll just have to clean up after him. Can't let him go outside until he has slept in the house.'

I could not see why Peter should get lost, after all, we were here, weren't we? Grandma further enlightened me: 'Makes no difference us being here. The first thing he'll do is try to find his old home. Cats always do. I know of cats that have walked hundreds of miles and ended up in their old homes.' In the event Peter solved the problem all by himself. As soon as he was released from the hateful basket he shot madly around the place and landed in the drip tray of the umbrella stand. There he saw to his needs to his great satisfaction. How clever of him, but then of course he was a pedigree Persian and they always know what to do in an emergency, they think for themselves.

We praised him and gave him the remainder of the milk which Grandma had brought with her for our tea. Then she decided to go to bed. She must have been very tired, I know I was. She said, 'I've made your bed in the back bedroom. We'll go up now. We must get up early tomorrow, there is so much to do'.

All the clocks had been stopped and the grandfather clock's weights had been removed, so there was no way of telling what time it was since Grandma had forgotten to wind up her watch. Upstairs I found three bedrooms. The front one was the largest with a view on to the houses across the road. Of the two back rooms mine was the bigger; the smaller room was set aside for Grandpa. Hardly large enough to hold a bed and a chair, poor Grandpa. I remembered Aunt Lily's comments.

Before getting into bed I stood entranced at the window from where I could see the length of the valley to the mountains beyond. It did not matter to me that the floor of that valley was littered with ugly mine shafts, piles of pit props and dirty slag heaps. I only saw the mountains, above, beyond, and all around. I did not feel shut in by them. To me they were friendly, sheltering, protective. In the immediate years I grew to love them, and, when hurt by life's frustrations, I walked them away on the mountains. When I reached the highest places the wind sang symphonies about my ears.

Chapter 14

When I awoke the next morning I could hear Grandma moving around. She was putting her bedroom straight. 'I wonder what the time is, it has been light for a long while. Must be getting on now.' We looked out of the back window. The sun was already well up into the sky and gave promise of another long hot day. A peculiar sound reached our ears. As we watched, a train came by on the tracks across the other side of the river. No ordinary train this. A seemingly endless string of coal trucks drawn along by a dirty old engine. There was something in the trucks, at first glance we thought it must be pit props. Then we realised that the trucks were packed with men. We could see their white faces above the tops of the truck sides. They were singing.

We later found out that men living some distance from the coal face might wait and be picked up at the coal sheds or along the track and transported to work in the empty trucks as they returned to the pit to be refilled. A loud hooter sounded, obviously the signal for the men now below the earth to come up and change places with these early songsters who would in turn be shut away from the daylight for hours on end.

There was no sight yet of a milkman in the street so we did without our customary cup of tea and drank cool water, while Grandma listed the things we were going to need from the grocer's as soon as we could find one open. I wrote out the list and we both turned to and began putting the living room and kitchen into good working order. The living room was quite a good size, square and easy to furnish. There had been a pantry in one corner but it had been taken out and a complete new kitchen and pantry built on to the back of the house.

Grandma had brought the living room fireplace with her from our old home. A place had been left in the new kitchen for its instalment. This was going to be a boon in hot weather for it meant we would not need to light a fire in the living room to cook meals. Just across the yard, about three paces, a new flush lavatory had been fitted up, down two steps and we were in a small walled-in garden. Another two steps took us from there into the long garden which ran the length of the house, and a hedge along the bottom end separated it from the river.

There were some neglected fruit bushes and a rotting clothes line but that was all we could see. We wondered if the former occupant had been an old person, unable to cope with a garden, or perhaps just not interested. One thing was for certain sure, it was not going to remain that way. Grandma looked around at the wasted land. Nothing much in the walled garden either, except plenty of weeds. 'There's a lot of work to be done, but we shall get it done all in good time,' she said. It was quite obvious to me that she intended using every possible inch of that ground and planned to start immediately.

We heard the rattle of a milkman's cart. I rushed in for a jug and out through the front door in case we missed him. We bought a pint of milk and asked the time of day. 'Ten minutes to seven, mam, and I'll be around here every morning at this time, eight o'clock on Sundays.'

Not yet seven o'clock. Why, we must have been up since five at least. I was hungry but we thought it unlikely that any shops would be open as yet. Grandma made a pot of tea and we sat outside on the back step in the morning air, with Peter doing justice to a saucer of fresh milk. Grandma said it was awkward about food. If she had brought anything along in the furniture van it would have gone off in the heat. Before the days when domestic refrigerators became regarded as a necessity, food spoiled overnight, however careful you might be. As for flies, well, they thought summer was their harvest time and ruined many a joint or rasher of bacon, although we used muslin or wire covers for everything perishable and kept it in the coolest place we could find.

Grandma was checking the grocery list and I was looking for the shopping basket when a loud knock on the front door startled us. I opened the door to see two children standing there with a huge shopping bag between them. They must have had a struggle to get it to us. Grandma came out to see what the commotion was. They both spoke together as if they had not a minute left to live. The words tumbled out. 'We're Betty and Willie and our Dadda sent these.' 'Who is Dadda?' Grandma enquired. I learned of yet another uncle who, they said, would be down later with some eggs. 'We couldn't bring them in case we smashed them.'

Two more cousins, in this land of surprises. Grandma asked the children in while she turned out the contents of the straw bag. What had not been packed in there just did not matter. There were far more items than we should have been able to afford. Betty and Willie grabbed the empty bag and rushed off, calling breathlessly behind them, 'Can't stop. We'll be late for school and we've got another errand to do.' Their Dadda evidently did not believe in 'keeping a dog and barking himself'. That was another of Grandma's favourite sayings.

We hungrily ate a breakfast of crispy bacon and fried bread. Later in the day Uncle arrived with the promised eggs. He stayed long enough to help lay the linos and carpets and move the very heavy pieces of old furniture like the large wardrobes and the sideboard that were getting beyond Grandma's strength, although, of, course she would never have admitted it. I had found the curtains. They were too long for these windows but with the help of some scissors, needle and cotton, were very soon hung in place.

The house was at last taking on a look of home. I thought it was a quite beautiful home and wondered how we, who were always so poor, could have possibly become the proud owners of such a well-equipped and modern establishment. I eventually discovered that the house had been bought jointly by four of my uncles who lived within a radius of three miles and could be called upon at any time if needed. The old home had become too much for Grandma with its three storeys and so many stairs to climb. They, the uncles, thought it would solve all problems if they had Grandpa and Grandma near to them and found the house, thinking it would be a nice place for them to live out their remaining years. They had paid for all the alterations and decorations. All we had to do was just move in.

We soon found, however, that Grandma did not like the way in which the front door opened directly into the front room. 'No privacy,' she grumbled. 'Every johnny that comes to the door sees all you possess. I don't like people gaping at us.' The uncles sent a joiner along to do her bidding and it was not long before we had a passage from the front door to the living room door. This made the front room smaller but it was still quite large enough to take the piano, sofa, some easy chairs and the old what-not with all the bits of Goss china and various oddments from times past. With the familiar pictures hung, *A Famous Trojan Boy*, *The Light of the World* and *The Stag at Bay* took care of the walls while the old black marble clock took place of honour on the mantlepiece. It was furnished fit for a king.

In about a week or so Grandpa came down from Aunt Lily's and was duly installed in his little back bedroom. He did not make any comment and found that he could get up and down the stairs reasonably well if he took it slowly. Over the past years he had had to give up his allotment garden because he could no longer walk the distance. Here he was right on top of the job and could come in and out of the garden at will.

During the following week Grandma said, 'You'd better start going to school on Monday.' I had begun to enjoy freedom and she must have seen the dismay on my face: 'It's not a bit of good you pulling faces about it. I shall get into trouble if you don't go and you might as well get on with it.'

With fear and trepidation I stood outside the school on the following Monday morning waiting for Esther to come and take me in. It was a large school with separate buildings for Boys, Girls and Infants. Our schoolroom was in an annexe at the end of the Girls' playground. It was a long low corrugated iron structure, not very attractive on the outside. Inside, however, was quite different. Light airy classrooms with large low windows and walls decorated in cream and pastel green. The desks were not the monstrosities I had formerly been used to, great six-seaters where getting in and out usually involved scraping the shins, especially if you were called from your seat in a hurry. Here they were two-seater desks with easy access either side. They were arranged in rows of six from back to front, and every pupil could see the blackboard at any time without having to crane or strain the neck or screw up the eyes to see past the girl in front.

Instead of all having to line up in regimental style in the playground and march into school, everyone went in and sat at their desks to wait for the teacher. Some of the girls used the spare minutes to do a row of knitting, others just chatted with their neighbours until Teacher came to her desk and said, 'Good morning,' sat down and took the register. The long room was divided by a wide gangway. At one side there was Class A and at the other Class B. Having two classes so close together never distracted us. It must have been to the credit of our teachers that we were able to concentrate so well on the subject in hand.

We stood by Teacher's desk. 'Hello, and who are you?' Before I could reply Esther put in, 'Please, Miss, she's my cousin Lucy and she's come to live here and she wants to come to school with me.' Teacher duly took my name and address and said she hoped I would like being with the class. 'Where would you like to sit?' she asked. Esther again took command of the situation. 'Please, Miss, can she sit by me because she doesn't know anybody else here.' Adjustments were made to the seating arrangements and I found myself installed alongside Esther who seemed mighty pleased with the way she had handled things for us.

I settled down to take whatever the day had to offer and found myself becoming involved without realising it. I was relaxed and able to pay full attention to the lesson. Playtime came and in the yard I found myself surrounded by most of the class. A new girl was something of a novelty, I did not have quite the sing-song lilt of the valleys, coming as I had from the Border-land. Consequently I was a foreigner, and labelled 'Cockney'. I hastened to explain that Cockneys were only found in London and that I was not a Londoner. However, they persisted in calling me Cockney and asking me to say something so that they could laugh at my strange accent. Their laughter was not unkind, just born of curiosity. I did not mind being the centre of that kind of attention.

Perhaps things would not have gone so well for me had I not had Esther beside me to champion and escort me. We Welsh have often been accused of being a 'suspicious lot', but I prefer to think that we have an innate possessiveness towards this Land of ours. Considering how often it has been fought over in the past it is not altogether surprising. The Act of Union — 1535 — which incorporated Wales with England did little to dispel the fears of losing a precious heritage. Things may be different today, but that is the way it was when I went down to school in the valleys over sixty years ago. Most of the girls came from bi-lingual homes. English was only spoken in public places like shops or school but I had yet to discover the pitfalls of Welsh/English translation.

After the rough treatment I had experienced at my former school I found this place vastly different. Not only in the teaching methods but in the attitude of the teachers towards the pupils. They actually seemed to like children. By the end of my first week, I had made several new friends. Two in particular were still close friends when I left school.

The summer holidays came and for the first time in my life I was sorry. I knew I was going to miss the daily involvement, but my fears were things of the past. That was when I really began to enjoy school.

Chapter 15

During the long hot summer holiday Grandma decided it was time we now concentrated on the garden. The house was all straight and tidy and needed less attention.

Grandpa was already busy in his piece and well ahead with his plans. He promised a regular supply of fresh vegetables and salads next summer. The uncles came often, usually in the evenings, and took over the heavy digging and clearing of overgrown bramble shoots which invaded and intruded into the precious growing land. There was quite a lot that Grandpa could do in spite of his age: he fertilised, weeded and hoed, sang softly to himself as he planted and was happy. Indeed he seemed to take on a new lease of life. Comfortless though his bedroom was, he did not appear to care. He spent almost the whole of the day out in his territory and very soon the place took on that cared-for look which is the delight of good gardeners everywhere. The promise of fresh food in abundance came true, and Grandpa wrought some miracle with the withering fruit bushes which later yielded gooseberries and blackcurrants for jams and pies galore.

Grandma and I toiled and sweated under the hot summer sun and into the glorious autumn. We brought order and beauty to our little garden. She begged plants, roots and cuttings from around the neighbourhood, while I weeded, cleared and tied-up tender plants. Under her watchful eye I became a part in the creation of something lovely.

Up at the pit-head furnace-men shovelled out enormous clinkers from the fires which powered the mechanisms there. Grandma spotted them one day while we were out walking along the side of the mountain. She thought they would look just fine ranged along the top of the garden wall. She asked about it and the man said it was quite alright: we could have as many as we needed but we'd have to get them away by ourselves. They were large, awkward and jagged but not heavy. We carted them away, two each at a time, in huge straw bags, until we had a great pile in the yard. The clinkers came in amazing colours, blues, greens, browns, reds and greys, all mixed up. We fixed them along the wall: they enhanced the view and provided extra shelter for our precious garden.

As time went by I met a lot more cousins. There were four families. Uncles and aunts and large families were the recognised thing in those days. All told, there were about 24 children. They varied in age between newly-born and grown-ups. I never became closely involved with any of them and found my friends among school companions who were, like myself 'only children' with no brothers or sisters to play with or to

56

confide in. When school began after the holidays I went back full of enthusiasm and found myself doing as well as the rest, except of course for arithmetic and Welsh translation.

On Friday afternoons at school we had needlework lessons. Everyone was encouraged to bring something from home, something useful, not just school work. Two girls in my class were knitting dresses for themselves in white knitting silk. I thought this was most clever. I remembered the old school, how awful it was to sit and try making buttonholes, and various stitches in a small hard piece of calico. The cotton knotted and on hot days the old-fashioned steel needles rusted in your hands. Here, I learned to do embroidery, intricate richelieu work and drawn threadwork. I made the traycloths which even Grandma had to admit were very nice. It was these little experiences which gradually melted my awful inferiority complex.

On the way home from school we passed a pit shaft. I used to stand and watch the great fan wheel which drew the clean air down into the earth below to the miners. I became aware of death and its constant threat to these valley people who daily burrowed beneath the ground. Occasionally we would see a handful of men pushing along the wicker carriage, the ambulance. We knew that someone was inside, perhaps just injured, more often than not, killed. Pram-like, on high wheels, the contraption was long enough to lay the occupant full length and had a hood to keep the light off the face. Funerals frequently followed the use of the ambulance.

I was about 12 or 13 years of age I think when the subject of ghosts came up. Weird stories circulated around the classroom, or were told and retold in playtime. We frightened ourselves half to death. No one had actually seen one of these strange phenomena but always knew of someone who had or knew someone who knew someone else who had and so on. Such stories have a habit of taking more upon themselves than was originally intended, especially after the third of fourth telling.

Imaginations went rioting around. It is a wonder we did not die of fright ourselves. Fearful of the dark nights in case these ghoulish fiends came to our own bedsides we were yet intrigued by the subject. When Maggie Evans invited us to go and look at her little cousin Willie in his coffin we felt it was a challenge. Led on by fascination for the unknown, or perhaps morbid curiosity, three of us went. Maggie, myself, and another girl called Katie.

Maggie knocked on the front door. It was opened by a lady not known to Maggie who, putting on a suitably grave voice, said, 'Please we've come to see our Willie.' The lady looked us over in turn, then said, 'Well, I don't know. Who are you? Only relations are supposed to come in.' 'That's all right,' said Maggie. 'I'm his cousin and these are my friends who used to take him for walks,' she lied like a trooper.

Evidently impressed, the lady replied, 'Come on in then. Don't make a noise. His mam's upstairs trying to get a rest, poor dab.' 'Poor dab' was an everyday expression as one would say 'poor thing' or 'poor soul'.

We crept softly into the parlour. Beneath the window, supported by two chairs lay the coffin. Nearby, propped against the wall, stood the lid. The brass plate said simply:

'William Henry Morgan
Born October 4th 1916
Died June 17th 1924'

Fear left me as I looked down at him, a still small figure. How could anyone be afraid? Nearly eight years of age, yet hardly big enough to be a four-year-old. There was not much to be seen of Willie, except for the bluish-white face and tiny hands, such fragile hands, folded across his breast. There was a mysterious smile on his face, almost as if he'd found out something that we did not know. He lay there resplendent in new herringbone tweed Norfolk jacket and matching knickerbockers, with a grey cap on his head. Feet and legs were encased in long black woollen stockings and heavy laced-up boots. It was probably the first complete outfit he had had since he had been put into his baby garments at birth. Well, the Co-op was a blessing at these times, especially if you had been able to leave a bit of 'divi' in. I wondered who had put his clothes on. Had it been his mother and had she cried when she did it? The girls tugged at my elbow, 'Come on, Lucy.'

We went back out into the world of the living, where the sun shone hot and brilliant and there were no dark clouds in the sky. We did not talk much on the way home, just our usual farewell, 'So-long', when we parted. I could not remember having seen Willie during his lifetime, and I hoped that dreams of him would not haunt me now that he had died. I also hoped he would not have minded me going to see him for in my heart I felt that I had intruded.

Chapter 16

Coal governed, controlled, in fact, ruled life within the valley. If you scuffed at the ground beneath your feet you turned it up in black dust. When strong winds blew, gardens were covered in it. When it rained, black rivulets like tears ran down the mountain breasts. The people lived off it, by it, with it. Men died because of it. A miner happily singing his way to work or joking with his butties could be maimed for life or dead before the shift was over. Usually docile ponies could be startled in the confines of their working space, lash out with their hooves and injure their leaders.

Mr. Henry Jones lived across the road, opposite our house. His was a happy home, his wife and his mother shared the work and lavished their love on his only son with never a hint of 'mother-in-law' trouble. Miners were never well paid by any standards, yet they kept their homes together with love and pride. Furniture gleamed from years of devoted polishing, and brasses, ranged along the mantle top, reflected borrowed light from coal fires in the evening. Tables were scrubbed until they could not possibly be made whiter, the weekly wash still came up like the driven snow.

William Henry was ten-years-old, always given his full name. Grandma said they made their house their God and William Henry was spoiled. 'Time would tell,' she said. They were making a rod for their backs. I liked William Henry. He too was an 'only child' and given to doing a lot of reading. He was the proud owner of a full set of children's encyclopaedias. He lent them to me one at a time: in return I lent him my annuals, *Tiger Tim, Pip Squeak and Wilfred,* and *Blackies.* Together we did the puzzles, exchanged riddles and found a lot to laugh about.

Suddenly, tragically, it all ended. Mr. Jones was brought home in the ambulance one afternoon. His companions said that he had been kicked by a pony, he was in dreadful pain. They laid him on the couch and the doctor came. There was little that he could do and Mr. Jones died later the same day. The matter of compensation arose since the accident had occurred below ground. Two eminent doctors came, employees of the company no doubt. They would make an investigation.

The kitchen table was newly scrubbed and washed with Lysol. Everything that could be taken out of the kitchen was removed and the rest covered with freshly laundered sheets, also impregnated with Lysol, and the floor well scrubbed. There, on the kitchen table — that friendliest of all pieces of furniture, around which things great and small are settled daily, for it is the hub of daily life — the great men performed the *post-mortem* examination that was to establish the cause of death. Mr. Jones' kidneys were found to be bruised, but they decided that there was no conclusive evidence that the bruising had been caused by the hooves of a pony. The men who had brought the dead man home had not actually seen what happened. They only knew what Mr. Jones had told them when they found him lying beside the track. Compensation was therefore ruled out.

'Scandalous,' said Grandma. Everybody knew what had happened. It was a proper cover-up job. 'Well, that's that,' she said summing up. 'The owners beat you down in the end.' She meant, of course, the pit owners. The Jones moved away after the funeral so I did not see William Henry again. I missed him, he was my first close friend.

There were moments in my life when I wished I could have died, when Grandma's antics covered me with confusion. I remember vividly the electricity affair. We duly received and paid a bill for each quarter year. During the summer, when days were long and light, we used no electricity at all. If Grandma thought we needed a little extra light around bedtime she would bring out candles. In her eyes it was sheer extravagance to use something just because it was there.

At the end of one such period she was most annoyed to see that the company had sent her a bill. She turned to me, 'Wash your hands and put on your hat. Take this to the man in charge and say, "There has been a mistake. We haven't used any electricity this quarter." ' I took the offending article and she went on, 'See that you ask for the head man and ask him please to put it right.' The man at the office took time to patiently explain that, although we had used no electricity, it was laid on. There was a meter and all the wiring and therefore the bill, which was quite small, was in order. In fact we were paying a rent for the facility. Grandma flatly refused to pay up. At last they threatened her with a summons and said that the supply would be cut off if the bill was not met. Grandma handed the money over grudgingly and went about protesting long and loud about the robbers down there who made you pay for things you never had. She possessed a very stubborn streak which could make life rather uncomfortable. Many people came up against it; often it concerned me personally.

One of my grown-up cousins, Georgina, taught music and singing. I had had a few lessons at the piano when I was six-years-old but the teacher went away from the town and I practised on my own after that. I could play simple tunes and hymns. Georgina thought I was quite good and, knowing our poor circumstances, offered to teach me free of charge if I would take the lessons at her convenience. I went on Saturday afternoons while other girls were playing in the park or paying their penny to see the latest American film at the local cinema. Georgina decided that I should go in for exams. I had been doing test pieces and she thought that I stood a good chance of getting through. Grandma said: 'NO! If Lucy is as good as you say she is, then that will do. She can carry on from there and practise at home.' That was the end of lessons for me in spite of my tears and Georgina's pleas. I passed the exams. for Higher Grade Schools; again there was a firm 'NO! I'm not having you turned into one of those flighty young hussies getting airs and graces!'

Teacher was arranging a concert at school for the end of term. I had been practising with the other girls, learning a Welsh jig. We were told that we should need nice white dresss, white socks and black shoes so that we all looked the same. Grandma said, 'There's no money in this house for fripperies. It's nothing but a lot of extravagance.' I did not like to tell anyone that we had no money. If I had I daresay someone would have lent me the necessary attire. Instead, I pretended to turn awkward and said I did not want to be in the concert. Miss Williams was very upset, as well she might be. There was little time to find and train a substitute. I refused to give any other explanation and wept secretly in bed.

Grandpa's sciatica eventually got the better of him and he could no longer get up and down the stairs to see to his beloved garden. He remained shut up there in his room. Grandma refused to look after him, she said he was 'paying for his sins'. I took his meagre meals up to him on a tray and hot water for him to wash. I did my best to keep the room clean and tidy for him and when Grandma went out I would sit and talk to him. One day I found him in tears, his pain was much worse and he had no help. 'I can't live like this any more,' he said. 'It's more than a human can stand. Will you do an errand for me?' 'Yes, Grandpa.' 'Will you get a message up to your Uncle Henry, ask him to come and see me?'

I gave the message to Esther at school and she in turn passed it on to her father. Uncle Henry came that same night. He spent a long time shut up in Grandpa's room. Grandma was very annoyed because she could not hear what they were talking about. Uncle's visit was a complete surprise to her. The outcome was evident the following day when Uncle and Aunt came with a hired car and took Grandpa away to live with them. They gave him a bed and the comfort which he had been denied for so long. I went to see him once. There he was propped up in bed with papers to read and his favourite bulls-eyes to suck. I never saw him again. Grandma found out that I had gone and my legs smarted from the weals left by her cane. Grandma's wrath was something to be reckoned with. Soon after that Uncle sold up his business and moved the family up to Worcester. He had bought a small shop there. He said it would be something for his girls to come into when they left school.

Grandma still kept up the practice of visiting all the local chapels without becoming too deeply involved, although she really favoured the Congregational, known as the Tin Chapel. It was constructed with sheets of galvanised zinc and painted green, giving an air of a warehouse. Inside, however, it was bright and cheerful, furnished with pine pews arranged in two groups with a centre aisle. An organ was beyond their means and the singing was accompanied by a lady playing an upright piano. Wet weather brought problems. The rain pounding on the tin roof made it difficult to hear what the preacher said.

One Sunday evening we went to a Baptist chapel up near the school,

Bethania, I think it was called. We did not know until we were well seated that the service would be conducted entirely in the Welsh language. The place was packed from floor to ceiling. The atmosphere was electrifying, powerful, spiritual, yet there was a reverence without solemnity and long faces as in so many chapels where you felt it was a sin to smile. Here, the people seemed to be filled with joy just to be there. The old preacher got so carried away in his opening prayer that when Amen came he was no longer facing the congregation but the wall behind him. We did not understand a word of what was being said or sung, but, oh, the singing! It was glorious, uplifting, and remained within my head until I fell asleep in my bed.

Chapter 17

Grandpa was well over the age of ninety when he died. They did not tell Grandma straight away, although all the aunts and uncles attended the funeral. In later years when the bitterness had eaten further into her, and her mind began to play tricks, Grandma became as a little child. Once, in a moment of lucidity, she was heard to say plaintively, 'Never had a chance to say goodbye, no chance to say forgive.' After Grandpa went away she had become more irritable and harder to please than ever before. It seemed that nothing I ever did was right.

The longing that had lain beneath the surface arose again within me. I needed to see my mother. I had not been back to her since we had moved down into South Wales. It was considered too far and too expensive for me to go. Now there were just two of us and the house and garden easy to manage I had time to fill.

I walked for hours upon the mountains thinking of all the things I might do when I was grown-up and no longer under Grandma's thumb. I have stood upon a summit with the sun above me, mists curling below my feet, shutting out the valley with its dirty old mines and tiny miners' houses which looked like dolls' houses from that distance. Sounds were never blotted out, I could hear clearly the mothers calling in the children, the men shouting to each other across their allotment gardens. It was a different world up there, a place where you dwelt for a time steeped in imagination, conjuring up for yourself all manner of wonderful things. The winds blew strong across your ears, making music so beautiful, music that you never heard on earth.

Sometimes on a Saturday morning, when my jobs were finished, Grandma would say, 'Get yourself off up to Uncle Stanley's. I don't want you skulking around here all day, and see that you make yourself useful up there.' Uncle Stanley had a fair-sized shop, crammed from floor to ceiling with everything the housewife could want, from a baby's comforter to a pound of tea. He never did anything 'on tick'. 'Don't believe in that,' he would say. 'Must have principles.' It was against his principles to encourage anyone to get things the easy way. Such refusal might have lost a lesser man a customer but he stuck to his guns, and, to be honest, his shop was always busy and remained open longer hours than the rest of them. There was never any question of early closing or holidays except for the Holy days like Easter and Christmas. He never opened on Sundays, not even for an hour in the morning, like some of his contemporaries. 'People,' said Uncle, 'People who are foolish enough to forget their needs on a Saturday must go without on Sundays.' Then he would trot out the one about the foolish virgins who forgot the lamp oil. He really ought to have been in the army, or at any rate in charge of something where he could have put to good use his

A view of the Rhondda taken on the author's nostalgic return visit in 1971.

ability for dealing with the foolish. He would most likely have earned early promotion.

The shop was by no means small, only it seemed so with the amount of goods stored there. One squeezed past sacks of rice, flour, sugar and chicken corn to reach the fruit and jams or bottles of pop. Behind the counter, itself weighed down as it was with boxes of eye-catching gob-stoppers, liquorice boot-laces, sherbet fountains, to say nothing of the huge bowls of homemade pickles waiting to be served out in penny-worths, there was just enough room for Aunt, or Uncle or The Girl to serve and manage the till. If three customers were in at one time, it was not just difficult but a work of art to get out again. This was especially true if they were, like the majority of Welsh matrons, short and a little stout. It did not help matters either if they should happen to be carrying their youngest in a shawl, Welsh fashion. The shop door could never be fully opened on account of the sacks of potatoes that stood along the back wall, for there was nowhere else to put them. No one ever complained and it seemed that Uncle was well respected although a little feared by people because of his religion. Every sale was made to the accompaniment of a text or an admonishment from the Bible. In between times he would sing loudly in his rich baritone voice the revival hymns of that period.

I was in the shop one day helping Aunt to weigh and pack the sugar into stiff blue bags. She would measure and fill and I would fold in the tops neatly. Mrs. Evans came in with her little girl, who hid her face behind her mother's skirt. Uncle, whose eagle eye rarely missed anything, spotted her. 'What are you doing, eh?' he bellowed at the poor little thing. Her response was to get even closer in to her mother. 'Hiding behind your mammy, is it?' Mrs. Evans replied for her, 'She's shy. Come on out, Ceri *bach*, say hello to Mr. Morris.' Ceri declined and stuck her thumb into her mouth. Uncle, of course, had to pursue the matter. 'Rubbish, woman, rubbish! Only the guilty need to hide. What have you done, eh?' He raised his face heavenwards and said, 'Father forgive them for they know not what they do.' As Mrs. Evans and Ceri left the shop Uncle called after them, 'For the wicked shall flee from the wrath.'

The Girl, who was a kind of general factotum, helping out where lay the greatest need, would come down the steps from the house into the shop each day at exactly twelve o'clock. 'Please, Mr. Morris.' 'Yes, yes, Girl. Speak up now. Dare to be a Daniel. What is it?' 'Please, Mr. Morris, Mrs. Morris says will you come to dinner before it gets cold.' It was a daily ritual. Uncle would then leave the shop, saying something like, 'My cup runneth over,' or, 'The Lord has provided. Blessed be the name of the Lord.' Then he might sing his favourite hymn, 'I am coming Lord, coming now to Thee. Wash me, cleanse me in Thy blood that flows from Calvary.' The Girl — she was never addressed by any name, I supposed she must have had one, but it was just The Girl — would stay in the shop until Uncle returned, then we went for our dinner.

Aunt would leave us to get on with our dinner and join Uncle in the shop. Perhaps she thought that we needed a little time to talk about the things which interested young girls. Uncle and Aunt took only half an hour for their meals. Uncle maintained that to spend more time on a meal was just wasteful. Only sluggards wasted time. He was certainly no sluggard, neither was my aunt. Their every waking moment seemed filled with useful activity.

There were occasions when Uncle would shut himself up in the small back bedroom to wrestle with the Devil. It lasted about three days, or until he felt that he had purged his soul of sin. Whether it was a real sin or an imaginary one, the procedure was always the same. He could be heard calling out loudly to God to forgive the wretched sinner and rescue him from the Devil and his evil ways. No one dared to approach him. Aunt used to excuse his absence from the shop and tell customers that, 'Poor Mr. Morris is having one of his bad turns.' When at last Uncle emerged, gaunt and unshaven, Aunt would put him to bed and feed him up like a sick child. In due course he took his rightful place once more in the shop and the affair was never mentioned.

At the end of a busy day Aunt would pack a large bag full of groceries and vegetables for me to take home. This was in return for all the little jobs I had done. To tell the truth I was glad to have the opportunity of spending a full busy day with them. It was too quiet at home with only Grandma and myself. Aunt usually gave me a penny as well. This was so that I could ride home on the tram because the bag of food was large and heavy and the walk home almost three miles. If it was a nice summer evening I usually spent the penny at the Bracchi's, that was the name given to the Italians who had settled in the country and set themselves up in sweet shops where they could sell the delicious ice-cream for which they were famous.

My arms would be almost out of their sockets by the time I reached home but I felt it was worth it and the taste lingered around my tongue from the half-penny bar of chocolate and the half-penny wafer. I did not tell Grandma about this, she would have taken the money off me and put it away. I felt I deserved a treat now and then. One night I nearly got caught out in my deceit. Grandma came to meet me. It was a nice evening and she felt like a walk out. I had just finished the ice-cream and had slipped the chocolate bar into the bag. When Grandma unpacked the bag later on she found the chocolate and gave it to me to eat. She would, of course, suppose that Aunt had put it in with the rest of the things. It must have been my guilty conscience that robbed me of the feeling of pleasure I usually experienced in the eating.

Chapter 18

Mr. Harries had a very large family, nothing unusual about that of course. Most people had large families. In fact, it was more usual than having just one or two children in a family.

He was a useful man to know. Not only did he sell all manner of household goods and equipment. He could also fit things up for you. He would bring a new light-bulb or gas mantle and perhaps a new lampshade to go with them. In a matter of minutes he would have them all fixed up, and no extra charge — providing you'd bought the items from him. I did not like him, there was something in the way he looked at you that put me off. His little piggy eyes seemed to bore right through you and made you feel guilty although you knew you had done nothing wrong. He was short and very fat. His ginger hair was always smarmed down close to his head with liberal applications of strange-smelling brilliantine. If I had to go up to his shop for anything I always hurried out as quickly as I could. Not that he would have done anything to me that was unkind, although his voice and manner were rather sharp at times.

I had never been to the seaside and when one day Mr. Harries was in putting a washer on the tap he said, 'I'm taking the children to Aberavonn tomorrow. I'll take Lucy if you like, but she'll have to be at the station by ten o'clock.' Grandma thought it was a heaven-sent opportunity for me to have a nice outing. 'There now, well, what do you say?' 'Thank you very much,' I replied with less enthusiasm than was expected. When Mr. Harries had gone Grandma said she thought I sounded as if I didn't want to go. 'I don't like Mr. Harries. He stares at me,' I said. 'Good gracious, is that all? Well, a cat may look at a queen I suppose. There's not much wrong with him, he looks after his wife and family. I know they go short of nothing.'

To look after the wife and family was her yardstick when it came to measuring up men. She went on about it. 'You'll have to learn that we are not all alike in this world. If you don't like the man put your pride in your pocket and make the best of it.' Grandma was very fond of that expression. If you had a raging toothache she'd say, 'Oh, put it in your pocket and forget it. Wait until you're a woman, then you'll know what pain is.' Later in a somewhat different frame of mind she said, 'There are times when one needs to hold the candle for the devil. Sometimes be civil to the uncivil.' I was not quite sure what that meant but supposed it was just trying to put up with things as usual

Aberavonn was old long before Port Talbot reared its ugly chimneys to supply the great steelworks. It was the nearest seaside town to us and on a direct rail link. The fact that I had never been to the sea did not mean that I did not know what it looked like. I had plenty of story books full of pictures to enlighten me. They were brightly coloured with brown-skinned children making sand castles under a cloudless sky of blue or running races at the water's edge. The sand was littered with shells and fronds of green seaweed. Oh yes, of course I knew what the seaside would be like.

It was early May and it rained. Dreary misty drizzling rain. My best pink wool cloth coat smelt steamy by the time I reached the railway station. Mr. Harries was superintending operations. I ran up to him and got in line with the rest of the children. He glowered at me, 'Come on, you're late, nearly went without you we did.' Mrs. Harries was sitting on a platform seat nursing her youngest. Ceridwen, Ceri for short, was bawling loudly, she evidently did not like all this excitement. She was only six-months-old. Mrs. Harries had a new baby almost every year. Ceri was number thirteen.

Mair and Arianwen were the two oldest. It was their job to see to the children who came in between themselves and the baby. They were a noisy lot and did very much as they pleased until their mother saw something which did not please, then she would complain in a whining tone to her husband. Mr. Harries would quickly assert his authority, cuff the offender around the ears and give them all a good talking to. With such a brood it was necessary for Mrs. Harries to have some help. They had a maid, Daisy. 'Poor Daisy' Grandma called her, for she was never done with weeping and her eyelids were permanently red and swollen with tears. Mrs. Harries put upon her, Mr. Harries shouted at her and the children teased and tormented her endlessly and mercilessly. She shared a bedroom with the toddlers and had many a disturbed night. She did all the dirtiest, most unenviable, tasks that others did not want to do. All this for a shilling to spend on Saturdays and three meals a day. I thought that if that had been me I'd have run away. Grandma said that Daisy had no place to run to.

The train came puffing in. I hung back a little from the group, looking hopefully for perhaps a compartment to myself. Any momentary ideas like that were swiftly put down. Mr. Harries made it abundantly clear that he did not trust anyone out of his sight. Into a compartment built for ten people, five a side, he packed the lot of us, seventeen! Talk about sardines! Big girls nursed little girls and the boys fought each other for window space. Mrs. Harries was even fatter than her husband and between the two of them they took up almost four seats. I was wedged in so tightly that I could hardly breathe and could not see past Mair who had little Myfanwy on her lap. Daisy had charge of the carrier bags with the food and a large straw bag with the bottles of pop. Fortunately the journey was not a long one and it was with great relief I felt the train slow down and come to a stop. I decided to sit still until the others had got out. Daisy held back as well and followed me.

Mr. Harries was the first to get out, his wife then handed down the baby to him. She very carefully and somewhat painfully manipulated her body through the narrow doorway and out of the carriage. The littlest children were lifted out, the big ones came out on their own, all except Arwell who fell out, true to his usual form. Daisy was the last to emerge and somehow she was unfortunate enough to get one of the carrier bags caught on the latch of the train door. The more she struggled the tighter it held. Mr. Harries shouted, Arwell howled and the poor baby, no doubt overcome by the whole terrifying experience, began to wail again. It was some time before peace was restored. By that time the bottom had fallen out of the unlucky carrier bag. We saved most of the food but a few buns rolled away on to the tracks beneath the train.

Mr. Harries marched us all out of the station. The ticket collector probably thought we were on a Sunday School outing party. It was not raining here but the sky was leaden as we trooped around the corner. Jenny and David sat down on the pavement and removed their shoes and socks. Arianwen gave a yell, 'There it is!' and rushed out to what looked to me like a muddy river. I turned to Mair. 'Where is the sea?' I innocently asked. She looked at me with disgust and disapproval, 'This *is* the sea, you fool.'

Mr. Harries went into the only shop in sight and doled out the cost of thirteen buckets and thirteen spades. The buckets were no bigger than teacups and the spades like wooden spoons. The whole lot cost him the grand total of three shillings and fourpence. I'm not much good at arithmetic but I think that would be the equivalent of seventeen or eighteen pence in today's currency. The day remained cold and overcast throughout. I kept my coat on all day and could not understand how the others could leave off half of their clothing and still look so happy. Arwell broke his spade and made such a fuss that Mrs. Harries said to me, 'Let him have your spade. He's only a little boy and you are a big girl.'

Going back home in the train everyone was tired and there was a row over a bar of chocolate. Mrs. Harries swore she had packed the right amount for everyone to get one. Someone had got at them. Mr. Harries thought it had to be me. Not one of his children would do such a mean trick as to steal a little bar of chocolate. Red-faced and confused, I could have wept, wedged again into a corner from which there was no escape. There was accusation in their eyes. I had a good idea who the culprit was but it would have been hard to make anyone believe me even if I had had the courage to speak up. What with all that fuss and the fact that the sea had not been blue, but grey like the sky, and the sun had not even peered out once during the day, the whole thing had been a flop as far as I was concerned.

Disillusionment comes hard to the young. When I eventually reached home Grandma was waiting all agog to hear what the day out had been like and had I enjoyed myself. I replied with little enthusiasm, 'Yes, thank you.' From that day onwards, however, I ceased to believe all that is written in story books and viewed the pictures with a critical eye.

Chapter 19

I left school in the year 1926. That was the year of the General Strike. The time when the great pit fan stopped turning. The pits were still, silent places. Women and children grovelled on waste tips to find some coal to keep their fires burning. Some of the men sold what their families had managed to glean. The penalty if caught was drastic. Prison sentences then were vastly different from those of today. Such transactions were therefore carried out after dark. They got precious little out of it. Most people would not pay more than a shilling for a bag, if indeed as much. Strange how we exploit the needy.

It was a long hot summer and the boys who should have been following their fathers down the pits for the first time welcomed the reprieve, not yet ready for the worries and responsibilities of the working man's life. They built up a dam across the little river and trapped enough water to make a swimming pool. There, in improvised swimming trunks and costumes, the boys and girls frolicked throughout the hours of daylight. Older people shook their heads, they disapproved: 'All that playing about will lead to trouble later.' Their remarks were, of course, ignored and the young played on, enjoying what life had to offer while there yet was time.

A new family moved into the house next door. They were Londoners who kept themselves to themselves. Perhaps they held back from making any new friends because it was a different kind of environment or they did not quite know how to approach their Welsh neighbours, who were wary of strangers anyway. We eventually discovered that Mr. Hopkins had been out of work and depressed because he could not support a wife and three daughters. He had taken the plunge and sold up the home to come to Wales where he had heard that there was work in the pits for anyone who might care to take it up.

Stories went around of him being seen in the doctor's surgery having treatment for blistered feet and lacerated hands. Whatever he had done in the past, it could not have been manual work. They did not use their garden except when Mrs. Hopkins hung out the washing. Then Grandma would contrive to draw her into conversation but it was brief and usually only to remark on the weather. In the hot summer when everyone else was outside, or sitting with the doors and windows open trying to keep cool, they shut themselves away. You never heard them talking to each other or heard any of the normal sounds which emanate between adjoining houses.

The two older girls went back to London as soon as they left school. They came down at holiday times and scandalised everyone with the underwear they hung on the washing line. Cami-knickers in mauve silk trimmed with deep lace had hitherto only been seen on the films, or displayed in the very modern shops and shown in the windows, 'As worn by Miss Theda Bara', who was an American film star. Their dresses were very short and their hair cut in the latest bobbed or shingled styles. Grandma said it was wicked the way they painted their faces and flaunted themselves. 'Flighty hussies,' she called them. Well, people had only just become used to women showing their ankles and were not yet ready for such forwardness. The youngest girl was not quite as old as me and still at school. She was very quiet and spoke when spoken to but did not make friends. At home she scuttled away inside her front door like a frightened little rabbit seeking the shelter of the warren.

The strike must have been the last straw for the poor man, for one night he hanged himself in the pantry. The two daughters came down from London and saw to the funeral arrangements, then took their mother and sister with all their belongings back to their native city. 'All for the best,' said Grandma. Suicide was looked upon as wicked; it was a crime then. There was little, if any, sympathy for the dead man or his family, shocked and stunned as they must have been at the tragic turn of events.

I was bored, life was far too quiet, the house was easy to look after and so were the gardens. I had a lot of time on my hands. Grandma had one of her brilliant ideas: 'It's high time you found something useful to do. I'll have a look around and see if there isn't a dressmaker that can take you on as apprentice.'

Sewing had always been a necessary job, helping with mending, or making new clothes for my dolls. I often had good ideas of my own in a creative way but it was definitely not my idea of a full-time occupation. I was quite happy when Grandma's scheme came to nothing. Dressmakers were an independent lot, a race apart with preconceived ideas about apprentices. They did not believe in giving away secrets or acting as tutors to the young without some financial recompense. They required prospective apprentices to pay for tuition. A lump sum could be agreed upon or in certain circumstances a weekly payment of, say, one shilling and threepence. This stumped Grandma, she had no money to give away. She thought, quite reasonably, that as the said juvenile would be doing all the tedious work, thus furthering the interests of the tutor, it should be paid for.

I began to go out every day, walking upon my mountains where I would dream of 'one day', some far off mysterious time when I should be rich and famous. Which of the arts would eventually carry me to that glorious state I had not as then made up my mind. If I had not been so painfully shy it might have been singing.

From the mountainside I saw the great Eisteddfod. Eisteddfodau in that era were superbly, totally, Welsh. A national event moving around the country year to year, giving everyone a chance to take some part. From my vantage point high above the small arena and the roped-off section for visitors and ticket holders I joined in or listened to the songs I had learned earlier at school. Lloyd George was there to present the awards and to chair the new Bard. People came from far and wide, bringing an air of joy, the joy of Welsh people when they meet in festival. For a brief space businesses boomed in the little Rhondda town. All the hard work, the practising on cold dreary winter nights paid off. School children by the hundred, choirs galore, poets, all took their turn and knew their moment of glory, for it was a great and glorious day.

Grandma said she had not been feeling well for a long time. She went to see a faith healer on the other side of the valley at Ferndale. This lady was blind and worked with a friend who measured out and packed up the herbs used in the various medicines. A lock of hair was asked for which the healer rubbed between her fingers, then gave her diagnosis. Grandma's blood had turned to water, she said. I suppose this was what we today would call anaemia, but that word was not known then, at least not to us, even if it was to doctors. Packets of the herbs were boiled and strained off, the liquid to be taken in regular doses. Grandma gave me a little taste. I was immediately sick. The smell of the stuff boiling was enough to put one off. I did not know how she could bear to drink it. Although Grandma felt that the medicine did her a lot of good, she did not go back for more. As well as the ninepence for a packet there was a train fare to find and she did not think she could manage it again.

Looking back I realise now that she must have been ill, but, of course, with my childish naiveté I saw her as a nagging old woman. There was just nothing that I could do which was right. I ought to be out in the world earning a living, bringing in some money, trying to support her now. So I went out and found myself a job. The card in the shop window said:

WANTED: Clean honest girl for daily work
    No cooking.
APPLY: Mrs. R. Thomas, 20 Clarence Street

I found the house and knocked on the door. My heart thumped and I half hoped that the door would not open. It was the first time in my life that I had done anything so important without asking Grandma first about it. She had never encouraged me to use my own initiative. Mrs. Thomas asked me inside. The house was bigger than ours, the furniture was very new and very modern. I was led through to the back of the house, the kitchen. She looked me up and down and asked me some questions. I must have given the right answers for she said, 'You are small for your age, you don't look very strong but you seem rather bright. I'll take you on a month's trial. Come along on Monday morning at a quarter to seven and I'll show you what I want you to do. You will get three meals a day and half-a-crown on Saturdays.'

Grandma seemed rather amused to think that I had got myself a job. I think she was pleased but was not going to say: 'I don't think the money is very good, but I suppose getting your meals there is a consideration. We'll have to see how it goes.'

Chapter 20

I presented myself for work on the Monday morning and was let in by Mrs. Thomas. There was a fire going in the huge old-fashioned range and a kettle singing on the hob. She made a small pot of tea, told me to sit down, and poured out a cup for each of us. She was already seated, wearing a pink satin dressing gown. I thought that that was rather forward of her. I understood from Grandma that dressing gowns were not to be seen outside of bedrooms unless one was ill.

My general instructions came quick and sharp: 'I'll give you a key to the front door so that you can let yourself in when you come. Your first job will be to clean the range, light the fire and boil the kettle. Mr. Thomas and I will have our tea in bed not later than seven thirty. If the fire is slow you may boil the kettle on the gas ring in the scullery, but only if it is absolutely necessary. I like to keep the gas bill as low as possible.'

I was looking at the great range and wondering how I'd ever get it cleaned and operating by eight o'clock, never mind half past seven. However, my employer had plenty more for me to do. Whilst Mr. and Mrs. Thomas were enjoying their tea in bed and preparing themselves for a new day, I would be 'doing' the front step and porch, then clean out the fireplace in the Lounge - they could not bring themselves to have a parlour or sitting room like everyone else — lay the fire and dust and tidy the room. This meant brushing the carpet and mopping the surrounds which were polished wood. Have own breakfast in scullery, all meals cooked by Madam. Oh, that was another thing — always address her as 'Madam' and Mr. Thomas as 'Sir' when spoken to. Wash up the breakfast things, clean and tidy the scullery, sweep out or swill — according to its needs — the back yard and outside lavatory. Do the upstairs landings, stairs and bathroom. Tidy and dust Madam's bedroom, except on Fridays when it had a good turn out. This applied to all the rooms, each having its own special day. Madam helped with this work. Have own dinner in scullery, half an hour allowed for sit down. Wash up, wash self, put on clean pinny in case Madam requires you to answer the front door. Do errands or any other little thing that Madam can think up for you. Have own tea, lay tea in kitchen for Sir and Madam. Sir comes home at six o'clock. Go home at five thirty, perhaps I should have said stagger home! Being new to such a routine and so much work I never finished the jobs as quickly as Madam would have liked. Often I had to carry some work over into the afternoon, but she did not say much about it. She did once remark, 'You are very slow, but you are thorough.' I took that as more of a compliment than a complaint.

Sir worked in the local Gas offices, Madam's father was some kind of an official up at the pit, and Madam had ideas far above her station in life. Her main ambition was to get rich quick, the quicker the better. She needed this in order to give herself all those little luxuries she felt she should rightfully have. I have not mentioned the 'Middle Room'. It was not part of my job to clean in there. It was Madam's shop. She sold ladies' wear to her friends and acquaintances , and other items of jewellery, fine china and handbags. She did not allow me to touch anything in there because some of the china and porcelain was very beautiful and very expensive. Sometimes when she went out I would creep in to have a look around. It was a veritable Aladdin's cave. A regular stream of customers came to try on garments or purchase a gift from the treasures there. I thought it was a splendid idea, having a little shop like that. When I told Grandma about it, however, she had very different views. 'Backroom trade,' she said. 'Backroom traders. Ought to be stopped.' 'But why? She has a lot of customers.' 'Oh I've no doubt about that,' replied Grandma in disgust, 'but it's cheating and should be reported to the proper authorities.'

I still did not understand her attitude: 'They are taking the bread out of the mouths of good honest business men. Hiding away their shops in back rooms so that they don't have to pay rates.' I had not known about that. She went on, 'Honest shopkeepers have to try to make a decent living and pay the shop rates. People like her don't need the money, it's just greed and should be reported.' I thought it best not to bring the subject up again in case Grandma got really inflamed about it and did something positive. She was, of course, thinking about her own sons, and the way they had worked to get established in their own businesses, good honest men.

I kept my job right throughout the winter and up to the following spring. The good effect that good regular meals should have had was quickly broken away by the amount of hard work and running about I had to do. I began to get very tired and Grandma sometimes had difficulty in rousing me in the mornings. Scared of being late, I would run off without a hot drink, snatching a couple of biscuits to eat on the way. She got cross about it: 'It's worse than slavery. Poor we might be but we don't need this. You had better leave, give in your notice before you make yourself really ill.'

I gave in notice in fear and trembling. Madam just could not believe her ears: 'Leave, leave a good steady job?' She gave me a new hat from her 'spring collection', and tried other ways to coax me to stay on. When it came to Saturday night I said firmly that I would not be coming any more. 'Grandma won't let me,' I excused myself. Madam laughed out loud. 'Won't let you?' she said as if it were all a joke. 'Why, what can she do? She can't stop you if you want to come.' Fishing around in my mind for a suitable reply I said, 'Grandma is going to report you for dodging the rates with your shop in the back room.' A look of paralysed shock spread over her face. I just picked my half-crown up from the table and ran before Madam forgot she was a lady.

I looked for another situation, but all in vain. Places were few and far between. Not many people in our little town could afford to keep a daily maid. Those who could usually had a cousin or elderly aunt ready to fill the gap. The days went by and Grandma became more and more irritable, she seemed to take delight in saying hurtful things, unkind things. She taunted me about being unable to find work. Heaven knows I tried, if only to get away from her for a few hours. The rift that had always been there, though lightly patched over, now became a gaping chasm between us. I became more unhappy and longed for the unattainable. I wanted to be where a plum tree cast its shade over a little flower garden, and the tall elder tree stood in a quiet dignity, every part

74

of it a gift to man. Where a laurel bush and a bay tree graced the communal burial ground of birds, cats and other small creatures long deceased. I remembered again bright mornings of waking up to love and laughter, if only —

One Friday morning I reached breaking point. Grandma went off to the shops for the weekly groceries and I made the big decision. The box where gifts of money received from aunts and friends were placed contained thirty shillings. I took half and put the box back in its place. I felt justified in taking money because it had been given to me, yet I also felt a thief.

I packed a change of underclothes into a small case and decided to wear my navy school mac in case the rain got heavier; it was drizzling then. I left the house in a state of indecision. I knew what I wanted to do, yet wavered. Time forgotten, I wandered on the mountainside, trying to make up my mind about my problem and hoping that perhaps some miracle would open up some easy way out. There was no miracle. My friendly haunt became my Gethsemane. In the late afternoon I went down to the railway station and bought myself a ticket. It was a long time since breakfast. I was hungry and bought a large block of chocolate. I had no fears about the journey, I knew which train to catch and that when it reached Quakers Yard I should have to change. I waited for the train to come and ate some of my chocolate but, being unused to much sweet stuff, I felt sickly and put the rest of it away in my case.

The train came, I boarded it, found a seat and settled down, beginning to enjoy my great adventure. We reached the large junction where people might get a train to any part of the country. I got out and asked a porter which platform I needed to be on for my connection. He looked at my ticket — half fare — and studied it and me, then said, 'Are you all alone, miss?' 'Yes, but I'm going home to my mother,' I said. He seemed reassured and said, 'Cross over that bridge and wait on the platform across there. The train will be in in half an hour.' I followed his instructions feeling rather pleased at having got this far without mishap. The train came thundering in and I got on. It was a corridor train and I chose an empty compartment. In a little while more people got in. Nobody spoke to me, I did not mind. I was used to being ignored and did not want to talk anyway.

The train left the station after much banging of doors and we soon picked up speed, rushing past little stations and never once stopping. It was all taking much longer than I remembered, but I suppose I had really forgotten, it was a long time since I had last travelled that way. Still no one spoke to me, and the evening began to wane, dusk drew on. The train still went rushing along!

Chapter 21

The ticket collector came along, everyone held out their tickets for inspection. He handed them all back smilingly. Not mine! He turned it over and over examining it carefully, then said, 'Where do you think you are going, miss?' I told him, he was silent for a few minutes, at least it seemed like minutes. With his disapproving voice he shattered my dreams completely with his next statement. 'This train is going to London. We've just passed Reading.'

He had another look at my ticket, then, 'I'll have to see about this,' he said and went away with my scrap of cardboard. I sank back into my seat wishing the earth would swallow me up. Suddenly everyone else in the compartment was staring at me. They seemed to be saying, 'Who is this person? How dare she do this awful thing?'

A tall well-dressed gentleman entered the compartment. He sat beside me and his voice was soft and gentle. 'You have got on the wrong train,' he said. 'Never mind. I expect you are hungry. Come with me and have something to eat.' He took me away from the staring eyes and sat me at a table in the dining car. There he bought me a glass of milk and a slice of fruitcake. I was grateful for the milk but the cake took a lot of eating. There seemed to be a lump in my throat which made swallowing difficult. My new friend talked to me, asked me questions, tried to persuade me to tell him how I came to be in this sorry predicament. After a while he took me back to the compartment and said, 'Stay there and don't worry. I will come and fetch you when we get into Paddington. Then we'll see what can be done.'

At first I felt relieved that things were not going to turn out so bad, at least I had found someone who could help me. Then ugly thoughts of remembered conversations crept into my mind. Men were bad creatures, only out to do you wrong. Grandma had instilled into me the need to steer clear of them. 'Not to be trusted,' she said. 'To be avoided if possible.'

Looking back I suppose the man was a detective with only my best interests at heart. I did not feel that I ought to go with him and when the train finally reached its destination I panicked, got quickly out of the compartment, and , once on the platform, began to run. Heaven knows where to, for I had not given any thought to what I ought to do or where I should go. Suddenly strong hands held me back. I had run straight into the arms of a huge policeman.

'Whoa there a minute.' His big hand held mine and he led me into the police station that is, or was then, part of Paddington Station, the place that criminals are taken in for questioning. I had not thought of myself as a criminal, but the Station Sergeant obviously did. As I stood before his desk, cold, tired and very frightened, he fired questions at me giving no indication that he believed my answers. He was also very annoyed with me and grumbled to the other men who sat around a dying fire. 'I'm sick and tired of these kids who run away from home. This is the third from the Rhondda this week.'

At last I managed to impress him by giving the names and address of an aunt and uncle who lived in Alexandra Park Road, Finsbury. The Sergeant asked me where my uncle worked. 'Maples of Tottenham Court Road,' I replied. He said in a loud voice, 'You are making all this up, aren't you. It is not the truth, is it?' I dissolved into tears and one of the other policemen led me to a chair by the fireplace where the fire was now almost out and the ashes were right under the bars. He asked me rather kindly, 'Would you like a cup of cocoa, miss?' 'No, thank you,' I sobbed in my desolation. With its dark green painted walls and bare floorboards the whole place was a picture of gloom and despondency calculated to strike fear and disillusionment into the hearts of even the most optimistic of persons, which I certainly was not at that moment. I sat there and waited, wondering what my fate would be.

Some time after midnight, a small grey-haired figure walked through the doors. Never was I more pleased to see her. My aunt looked at me in severe tones and said, 'Lucy, what are you doing here?' I could not find the words to reply and, severe though she sounded, Aunt was kindness itself. She took me home in a taxicab, made a bed up for me and tucked me in. 'Now then, young lady, you'd better get some sleep. No use talking tonight. We'll see what can be done tomorrow.'

Tomorrow, and the next tomorrow, indeed for the rest of that week, I was treated like a favoured visitor instead of as I had thought would be the case. I thought I would be treated like a wicked girl by this aunt to whom I had never been particularly close. Wherever she went I went too, shops, visiting friends, doing her stint at the Church Bazaar. I was drawn into conversations along with the grown-ups and made to feel that I belonged.

When I had been there a week Aunt Hilda came and took me to her place. She had married and was living in a flat. Uncle came from a large family, and people visited a lot in those days so the week was spent in making a lot of new friends. At the end of a fortnight they sent me back home to Grandma. I found out that the hardest part of running away was the going back. I did not want to go, but they were insistent. 'You must go back,' they said. 'For the time being at any rate. You must not get so upset at the things Grandma says to you. Her bark's worse than her bite. She's our mother and we know exactly what she is like.' She had always held up her daughters to me as two shining examples of what I ought to be. Had she then treated them in the same way that she treated me? That was something that had never before occurred to me.

Grandma met me off the train, she was very quiet, saying little throughout the evening and not once mentioning my escapade. Aunt Hilda had told me that Grandma had been very upset and worried when I had not come back to the house that fateful Friday. A policeman had called around midnight to tell her that I was safe and well and had turned up in London. I wondered what her thoughts must then have been.

For a little while things were not too bad between us but then the old longing returned. It was never far away, but this time I told Grandma about it. She became angry, although she must have know that it would happen. She stormed at me, 'Go on , then, go to your mother. You'd better write and ask her to fetch you. You might get on the wrong train.'

I felt a bit sore about that mistake but had no regret for what I had done, and, after all, I had had the best holiday I had ever had. I wrote to Mother, just a short letter to ask if I might live with her, and please would she come and fetch me.

Mother sent a telegram to say she was coming the next day. She must have read beteen the lines, she knew where my heart lay. She brought my younger sister with her and Grandma lost no time in being unkind to both of them. Then it was, 'I took her in, brought her up, fed and clothed her all these years and now just when she could be useful to me

Lucy aged about 13 with her Aunt Hilda.

you are taking her back.' I felt rather bad about it because it had been me who had stirred the whole thing up in the first place. Mother was very calm about the situation; 'Don't worry, my dear, we'll be out of here tomorrow morning.' She had to stay the night and we were catching an early train the next morning. In the morning I began to collect up some books and music. Grandma came in and said, 'You put those all back. You'll take nothing out of this house but what you've got on.' That was how I went, nothing but the clothes I stood up in, not even one of my treasured books. 'Leave them,' said mother. 'There are plenty more where you are going.'

We turned back to wave when we reached the corner of the street but Grandma was still angry and shook her fist at us as a parting salute. If only she could have unbent a little, but perhaps she had forgotten how. Her pride was always such a stumbling block, and bitterness the weapon that finally destroyed her. Mother was quite philosophical about it all: 'Don't you get upset, my dear. Perhaps one day she'll get around to our way of thinking.'

Now I must put the past behind me. Although I had loved the little gardens and was leaving my dear friendly mountains, I knew that at last there was a better place for me. Indeed, what could there be better than to be at home, living each new day with my mother.

Epilogue

I visited briefly — a few hours only — the Rhondda in 1971. On high peaks I stood enraptured, gazing at the forest land, wooded slopes, and green pasture land reaching out to a distant horizon where misty blue mountains met the sky.

My family had never been there before and couldn't quite understand my eagerness to get out of the car time and time again, just to have a look. We passed lovely picnic parks among sheltering trees just off the busy road. Tree trunks, rough hewn and tops smoothed over, made seats and tables where the traveller might eat a packed meal in magnificent comfort.

Riding down to Cwmparc brought more nostalgic memories. I remembered the mountain before the road snaked its way across the green breast. I remember, too, the local interest and excitement when gangs of men began to cut and lay the foundations for this route which was to make access to the other side of the mountains so much easier. It also provided work for many men. Hard, gruelling work, yet no one ever complained. It put dinners on the tables of many near-starving families.

It was here in Cwmparc that I spent those last four years of my childhood before going to live with my mother. A high fence shut off the view of the long garden and we did not disturb the present occupants of the little house in Clare Road. I knew that the school around the corner up the hilly road would be closed and silent — it was summer holiday time. We turned in the other direction, on to Treherbert where we tracked down one of my long-lost but never-forgotten cousins.

There can be nothing in all the world like a real Welsh 'welcome home'. It does not matter how long you have been away, out comes the teapot, sandwiches and cakes appear as though by magic and you talk! Oh, how you talk! There is so much family news to catch up with. Reluctantly we had to leave with promises on both sides being extracted 'to keep in touch now'. It had truly been a day to remember. To take from the recesses of memory's store room gems to savour in quieter moments. To see again, although in retrospect, the verdant grass, the trees and lakes that grace the Land of my Fathers.